INSPECTING SCHOOLS

INSPECTING SCHOOLS

HOLDING SCHOOLS
TO ACCOUNT AND
HELPING SCHOOLS
TO IMPROVE

Brian Wilcox and **John Gray**

Open University Press
Buckingham • Philadelphia

Open University Press
Celtic Court
22 Ballmoor
Buckingham
MK18 1XW

and
1900 Frost Road, Suite 101
Bristol, PA 19007, USA

First Published 1996

A catalogue record of this book is available from the British Library

ISBN 0 335 19675 6 (hb) 0335 19674 8 (pb)

Library of Congress Cataloging-in-Publication Data
Wilcox. B. (Brian)
      Inspecting schools: holding schools to account & helping schools to improve/Brian Wilcox and John Gray.
          p. cm.
      Includes bibliographical references (p. 176) and indexes.
      ISBN 0 335 19675 6. ISBN 0 335 19674 8 (pbk.)
      1. School management and organization–Great Britain.
2. Educational evaluation–Great Britain. 3. School management and organization–Great Britain–Case studies. 4. Educational evaluation–Great Britain–Case Studies.
I. Gray, John (John Michael). 1948–   . II. Title.
LB2900.5.W55 1996
371.2'00941 dc20   95-50907
                                                                                               CIP

Typeset by Type Study, Scarborough
Printed and bound in Great Britain by
Biddles Ltd, Guildford and King's Lynn

To Jean and Julia,
Aidan and Vanessa

CONTENTS

PREFACE AND
ACKNOWLEDGEMENTS

When we first began to think about undertaking the research on which this book is based, public attention was squarely focused on the problems of introducing the National Curriculum and the testing programmes which accompanied it. Our interest in the nature and impact of inspection was considered by some to be slightly esoteric. We were already aware, however, that things were about to change. LEAs were being encouraged to develop more extensive programmes of school inspection and evaluation. Many were responding innovatively and we were interested in what they were doing. But, shortly after we had begun to set up our research, some of those close to central government began to show signs of impatience; LEAs were not, in their view, moving fast enough towards 'rigorous' models of inspection. New legislation was in the offing.

The 1992 Education Act was debated and passed through the House of Commons. New arrangements for inspection were proposed. Some resistance in the House of Lords brought a few concessions. Within a very short period of time, however, a new agency (the Office for Standards in Education, or OFSTED) had been set up, acquired a new Chief Inspector to lead it and 'trained' a new cohort of inspectors. A major nationally-organized programme of school inspections ensued.

We found ourselves in the unusual position of having started an extended programme of independent research whilst a 'revolution' (or at least its educational equivalent) was being launched around us. The LEA inspectors, schools and teachers with whom we were in contact were keen to tell us about their experiences.

This book is the main outcome of our research. We are particularly grateful to the Economic and Social Research Council for providing a grant to support it. Homerton College, Cambridge partially supported Brian Wilcox during the last phase of the project whilst Sheffield University offered other facilities.

Our main debt is to the LEAs and schools who gave so generously of their time to help us with the research. Some have told us that they would be happy to be identified; others, however, have not wished to be named. We have therefore decided to list those who helped merely by the pseudonyms we gave them.

The LEAs have been referred to as: Besford, Churdley, Falton, Folkshire, Forestshire, Loamshire, Middleshire, Mortdale and Sedley. Officers, inspectors and advisers in these authorities sustained their commitment to the research over years rather than months, despite changes in personnel and sea-changes in the jobs to which many of them had been recruited. Officers of two professional organizations, CAID (Centre for Adviser and Inspector Development) and NAIEA (National Association of Inspectors and Educational Advisers), also gave significant assistance during the early stages of the research.

We are equally grateful to the schools which participated in the project. As readers will discover, many of those we visited had not found the experience of being inspected particularly comfortable; indeed, in one or two cases they were in something akin to a state of shock since learning of the inspectors' conclusions. Yet, almost invariably, they treated our requests for information and clarification with integrity, giving generously of their time even when we were probing the most sensitive of issues.

The primary, middle and special schools in the project are referred to as: Austin Road, Broad Lane, Burnden, Coverley, Danbrook, Fenby, High Lees, Lowstone, Low Springs, Milton, Murbank, Playfair, Richardson, St Mark's, St Peter's and Trenton Storrs. The secondary schools are referred to as: Alderman King, Carlow, Ecclesley, Ladywell, Laurels, Low Moors, Midchester, Monkton, Potterton, Prince Edward, Strafford, Tennyson Road and Turner.

When we began our research we benefited from the informal advice and assistance offered by several members of Her Majesty's Inspectorate. We have also learnt a good deal from members of OFSTED and from the research they themselves have commissioned. Their willingness to share their thinking (often in print) with others in the profession has been striking.

Finally we need to say something about colleagues who helped us at various stages of the research. Professor Jon Nixon and Dr Pamela Poppleton both assisted with the case studies of individual schools whilst others in the QQSE (Qualitative and Quantitative Studies in Education) Research Group helped us to sharpen our ideas when we were starting. Jean Booker, Susan Round and Pauline Turner provided first-rate secretarial support at various stages. Brenda Finney skilfully managed our increasingly large database of interview material whilst Louisa Chapman brought a discerning eye to the preparation of the final manuscript.

John Gray and Brian Wilcox

1   INSPECTION: PROMISES AND CHALLENGES

The rise of inspection during the first half of the 1990s has been remarkable. We know of no educational commentator in the mid-1980s who had the foresight to predict its dominance. We ourselves began to think about a programme of research into inspection 'in all its forms' in the latter half of 1990. At the time it was clear to us that inspection was a developing force but we, along with many others, were taken by surprise at the speed with which events gathered pace.

The new system

The implementation of the Education (Schools) Act has changed profoundly the arrangements for the inspection of schools in England and Wales (DES 1992a). Previously inspection had been the exclusive preserve of the national inspectorate (Her Majesty's Inspectorate, known as HMI for short) and the inspectorates of the local education authorities. Basically HMI determined which schools would be inspected on a national basis whereas local inspections (where they occurred), were decided by the local education authority (LEA) and its inspectorate. The two systems were essentially independent of each other.[1] Under the new arrangements decisions about which schools are to be inspected are taken centrally by a new non-ministerial government body known as the Office for Standards in Education (in England and Wales) – universally referred to by its initials OFSTED.[2]

Inspection is now carried out by independent inspection teams, each led by a registered inspector (RgI or 'reggie' as they are colloquially known). RgIs and their teams may be employed by LEAs (still the majority), universities or private firms or, indeed, may be self-employed. In each inspection team there must also be at least one 'lay person' who has not been involved professionally in the provision or management of education. All inspectors must normally have completed an approved course of training.

The delivery of inspection has been radically reconstituted as a market in which the amount of work inspectors obtain depends on the outcomes of competitive tendering. The inspection teams work privately under contract to OFSTED.

The 1992 Act and subsequent regulations (DFE 1993b) require all schools to be inspected once every four years.[3] If this target is achieved some 6000 schools would be inspected annually – a volume of inspection which far exceeds that achieved previously (see Chapter 3). After an inspection the governing body of a school is required to produce an 'action plan' which sets out its intended procedures for implementing the inspection findings.

The model of inspection adopted is the most comprehensive ever and covers virtually all aspects of a school's activities. The document *Framework for the Inspection of Schools* (OFSTED 1992a, with subsequent revisions 1993a and 1994a) set out the scope, criteria and standards for inspection. This Framework is included as the first section of a *Handbook for the Inspection of Schools* (OFSTED 1992b; 1993b; 1994b) which provides detailed guidance on its application. Unlike previous such manuals copies of the Framework are made available to schools and the Handbook may be purchased by schools or, for that matter, anyone else.

As 1992 drew to a close the preparations for OFSTED were in place; it was already the dominant player on the inspection scene even before its first inspections had taken place. Secondary inspections began in September 1993. By the end of the school year 900 inspections had been completed. The primary and special school programmes began in September 1994. With some 20,000 primaries to inspect as well as the secondaries one would have anticipated some faltering in the pace but, after some initial doubts about whether enough inspectors with credible experience of primary schools could be recruited, the four-year programme was claimed to be getting back on schedule by the end of 1995. At the end of the four-year cycle not only would *every* school in England have been inspected once but a few (those in difficulty) would have been visited again to review progress since the previous visit (see Matthews and Smith 1995 for a more detailed account).

In brief, the system of inspection inaugurated by the 1992 Act represented an unprecedented attempt to apply a universal model of inspection of ambitious frequency and comprehensiveness, carried out by independent inspectors drawn from a wide range of backgrounds and operating on a competitive commercial basis. We doubt if any more ambitious programme of school-by-school evaluation and review has ever been mounted anywhere in the world.

The research base

The growing conviction that inspection 'works' has been impressive but, until recently, must have been based largely on faith or gut-feeling. As Roger Frost (a member of Her Majesty's Inspectorate) has observed, in a reflective piece on the nature of inspection, 'no serious mention of inspection has been made in the literature on school effectiveness' (Frost 1995: 3). He is, in our view, right to point to the obvious gaps in the knowledge base. However, this omission is not confined to this field of research alone or to the broader study of educational evaluation. To the best of our knowledge, whilst there were external reviews by governmental bodies of Her Majesty's Inspectorate *and* local inspectorates during the 1980s, none of these systematically investigated core assumptions about the 'effectiveness' of inspection either (see Chapter 3 for fuller details of such reviews).

We are not, of course, arguing that nothing was known about the probable effects of inspection during the period when its expansion was being mooted. We do not subscribe to that rather precious school of academic thought which implies that if something has not been thoroughly 'researched' (whatever that may mean) then little or nothing is established. A vast amount of experience *was* available, both nationally amongst members of HMI and locally amongst LEA inspectorates. It was doubtless tapped into as those charged with implementing the new arrangements set about tackling their brief. What we are suggesting is that the 'conventional wisdom' about how inspection worked (particularly in terms of its effects on individual schools and their subsequent improvement) was based on a set of at best partially tested assumptions. Influential people charged with implementing inspection programmes could, when challenged, provide us with insights into the ways inspection functioned in their experience; their accounts, however, were somewhat tentative (see Chapter 4). In the language of social science what they offered would best be described as *'plausible* hypotheses', likely to be borne out in practice but not certain.

In short, when decisions were being made about the importance of exposing all schools to systematic inspection on a regular basis the evidence base was not only very limited, in terms of the number of studies available, but also very restricted in terms of the core assumptions it had explored.[4] The move towards a comprehensive and national system of school inspection was something of an experiment. Those most closely engaged in conducting inspection have, perforce, done some of their learning on the job.[5]

This book is about the practice and development of the inspection of schools during the first half of the 1990s. It is centrally concerned with the experiences of those on the sharp end of inspection (teachers and schools) as well as some of those professionals responsible for managing them. The period can be conveniently divided into two phases: the period from around the time of the 1988 Education Reform Act up to the end of 1992, and the period since then. When historians come to write up the history of school evaluation they will doubtless refer to these as the 'pre-OFSTED' and 'OFSTED' eras.[6] It would be tempting, therefore, for readers to imagine that what we have written is an evaluation *of* OFSTED. We have undoubtedly written a lot *about* OFSTED but 'inspection' and 'OFSTED' are self-evidently not synonymous. Whilst there are several respects in which the introduction of OFSTED represented a radical break with previous practices there are many other ways in which it did not (see Chapter

4 for a detailed analysis). The continuities in practice over more than a century of school inspection are at least as impressive as the changes.

There is another reason why we prefer to take the broader view. We are confident that *school inspection* will still be with us when we enter the next millennium. The OFSTED agency, however, may by then have been judged to have completed its tasks or may have mutated into some other form.

Assumptions and prospects

Most accounts of inspection suggest that it serves two main functions in an educational system. The first set of claims relates to accountability and providing a picture of what is going on for decision-makers. Inspections can be aggregated to provide both a national and a local picture about the 'state of the system', identifying aspects of quality and standards as well as some of the gaps. As Frost put it: 'inspections have set a full agenda for secondary schooling in general and . . . reports on individual schools have set a similarly full but school-specific agenda' (1995: 2). Anthea Millett, OFSTED's first Director of Inspections, emphasized a similar view during the period running up to OFSTED's first inspections:

> Inspection can help . . . by creating the best-ever knowledge base about the educational service which will offer society a full account of how schools and pupils are doing throughout the country; and by providing assurance to tax-payers and politicians that public money is being spent and managed efficiently by schools. My hope is that inspection will come to be seen as a periodic staging-post in a school's development and that it will also be seen as a genuine partnership in which the inspector's visit is linked to the school's and community's own concerns and aspirations.
>
> (Millett 1993: 12)

The second set of claims concerns the influence of school inspection upon school improvement. How might this process work? Millett (1993) pointed out that OFSTED had adopted the phrase 'improvement through inspection' to sum up its corporate hopes. She also offered some 'pointers' as to how this might happen. The new inspections would be focused on 'standards of pupils' achievement and on how to raise those standards'. They were 'uniquely placed to bring about change where it matter[ed] – in the classroom':

> An acid test of a school is the standard and quality of pupils' learning in lessons. Skilled observation can throw into particularly sharp relief the highs and lows of pupils' school life – the magical, inspired or simply very competent lessons they experience as well as any moments of torpor, incomprehension or alienation.
>
> (Millett 1993: 12)

The strategy included the importance of greater parental involvement 'by ensuring that inspectors talk to parents and, more importantly, listen to them' and recognized the need to link 'inspection to action through action plans and schools' own development planning'. 'Improvement through inspection will remain just a slogan', she argued, 'unless the governors, heads and staff of schools actually take up (as they are required to do) the issues, address any weaknesses and build on the strengths' (Millett 1993: 12).

International interest in inspection

Aspects of inspection have attracted considerable interest from around the world. North Americans, for example, have seen it as a possible alternative to school evaluations based on the results of standardized tests. Indeed, one American researcher has gone so far as to describe it as 'a remarkably fresh way to view school assessment' (Wilson 1995). Echoing Millett's concern with class-room performance, he commented:

> Over its 150-year history, inspection has evolved a methodology that portrays and judges the quality of what actually happens in schools. Inspectors, who have been experienced teachers, actually visit schools, directly observe classes and make judgements about the quality of the teaching and learning based on the evidence they collect at the school. Through a team moderation process the judgements of individual inspectors are discussed and a corporate judgement is agreed upon by the inspection team. The results are reported back both to school people and policy-makers. Inspection has managed to keep the issues of quality, assessment and support of schools directly tied to schools and to provide consistent information both to policy-makers and school practitioners.
>
> (Wilson 1995: 95)

As a report from OECD researchers underlines, considerable investments in systems of inspection have been made in other countries as well as Britain with a view to ensuring higher standards of education.[7] In nearly every case the assumptions underlying the strategy have been similar. First, to make schools more accountable to the communities supporting them; and second, to put pressure on schools to improve (Brooks and Hirsch 1995). As one of the researchers summarized it:

> There are really only two ways of evaluating schools: inspection or review (that is actually visiting schools) and the use of performance indicators. Different countries use different combinations of the two methods.
>
> (*Times Educational Supplement* 1995: 16)

Criticisms and challenges

The explosion of interest in inspection methods (and the criticisms which have accompanied this interest) is a recent phenomenon. Despite the status and influence of HMI in the previous system, and the publication of reports on individual schools, there was comparatively little critical comment about either the nature or the impact of inspection. With the advent of OFSTED, however, all that has now changed. A number of criticisms have now been formulated of the inspection approach. Many of these apply to all inspection methods and should, perhaps, have been given greater attention in the past; others are more specifically about the particular procedures OFSTED has adopted or chosen to continue.

It is not our intention either to dwell long on these criticisms here or to give a blow-by-blow account of who has said precisely what. Our concern is merely to give some feel for their flavour and to point the interested reader towards some starting points. Most of the issues to which we ourselves attribute importance are tackled in greater depth in subsequent chapters. We discern several general concerns.

The methodologies of inspection

The first is about the methodology (or methodologies) of inspection. What do inspectors base their judgements on? Back in 1979 former Senior Chief Inspector Sheila Browne stated:

> The basic principle has always been close observation exercised with an open mind by persons with appropriate experience and a Framework of relevant principles.
>
> (Gray and Wilcox 1995: 50)

One is just as likely today to hear similar answers about inspection being based on what inspectors observe and see in classrooms. This evidence is then interpreted in a 'common-sense' way. There is just one problem with this stance – as any first-year student of social science knows, 'common sense' is not widely acknowledged to be a method. What one person finds straightforward another finds problematic – methods and values are inextricably entwined.[8]

Continuing in this vein critics have asked questions about how 'valid' and 'reliable' inspectors' judgements are. How do they attempt to achieve 'consistency' and to avoid 'subjectivity'? And are their approaches sufficiently 'rigorous' in weighing the strengths and weaknesses of different kinds of evidence? (See Maw 1995 and Fitz-Gibbon 1995 for entry points into these debates.) Such terms are drawn straight from the canon of social scientific method and have precise and technical meanings as well as 'common-sense' ones. Others have asked whether a 'snapshot' approach which attempts to capture everything that is salient about a school within a short time-space (usually a week) is up to the task of seeing where a school has come from, where it 'actually is' (the main concern currently of inspectors) and where it might be heading. Do teachers simply prepare for the inspection and 'put on a front' which masks reality? Primary schools, meanwhile, have been concerned that the inspection Framework may be too secondary-oriented in its assumptions.[9] There have also been continuing doubts about the extent to which inspectors, in forming their judgements, have been willing to take into account the specific 'contexts' within which schools are operating and, equally importantly, whether they are capable of doing so.[10]

Such questioning frequently engenders some defensiveness on the part of inspectors, often leads to assertions that inspection has broader concerns than the rather narrow ones of educational research, and so on. We find such responses somewhat unhelpful. The difficulties, in our view, arise in part from the lack of interchange between the two groups. If educational researchers were more familiar with the constraints under which inspection has to operate then they might be more understanding about the difficulties of taking certain criticisms about methodology on board. Conversely, if inspectors were more familiar with methodology then they might come to see that *some* changes in their taken-for-granted practices might be called for; indeed, a thorough knowledge of such issues might help them to focus their activities more clearly on what they believed to be really important. But some of these questions are not just ones inspectors should be considering. They are fundamental to the conduct of educational evaluation. And, as with most such questions, individuals may differ in what they consider to be appropriate responses. Whatever the merits of these different positions a securely based portrait of the school is a precondition for subsequent efforts to develop it. We attempt to steer our own way through these concerns in Chapters 4 and 6.

The effects of stress

A second set of concerns has to do with the impact of inspection activities on teachers. The effects on their morale and their subsequent enthusiasm (or lack of) for improvement efforts are central here. In the past the majority of teachers could get by with only a passing acquaintance with inspectors. Now all are forced to cope with them. The pressures and anxieties which such contacts may engender can be counter-productive, rhetoric to the contrary notwithstanding. High (and possibly dysfunctional) levels of stress may prevail. A 'Dunkirk spirit' may be engendered and 'I survived the inspection' T-shirts, or their equivalent, may proliferate (Brimblecombe *et al.* 1995a; Wragg and Brighouse 1995). Such responses could lead to teachers' failing to absorb the central messages of the inspectors' reports or somehow downgrading them into tasks for tomorrow.

Our own evidence suggests that inspection is (almost inevitably) bound to be 'a stressful experience' for those concerned (see Chapters 2, 5 and 8 for specific examples). The real challenge is to ensure that such stresses are minimized wherever possible and that the nervous energy which inspection engenders is captured for improvement. Our research underlines, however, many of the sensitivities and some of the obstacles. *How* one shows teachers the 'magical, inspired or simply very competent lessons' pupils have experienced and refers to the 'moments of torpor, incomprehension and alienation' is likely to be just as important as *what* one actually shows them. The language of inspectors' reports (with the veiled threats that are sometimes perceived) may not always produce the desired responses.[11] For teachers to be motivated the findings of an inspection report may need to be mixed with some vision.

The costs

One of the new areas inspectors have been asked to take on board as part of the OFSTED Framework is a series of questions about the efficiency with which schools deploy their resources and provide 'value for money'. A third set of concerns has focused on the extent to which the 'full inspection' model is itself cost-effective and producing insights which are worth the effort and expenditure they entail (see Clare 1994 for an attack along these lines). It has sometimes been described as a 'Rolls-Royce' model of inspection, prompting the question whether cheaper versions might not, in many cases, suffice.[12] Some have suggested alternatives (such as moderated self-evaluation) which are likely to cost a lot less per school, and others have proposed 'barebones' strategies focusing in the first instance simply on key statistics about performance (see Burchill 1995). It would be interesting to speculate how schools themselves might have used such sums (equivalent, in the case of a large secondary school, to the better part of a senior teacher's salary for a whole year), had they been given the opportunity.

Our research began at a time when what we have termed an experiment in 'inspection in all its forms' was taking place. Consequently we have some limited evidence with which to compare approaches (see Chapters 2 and 7). Two things in particular struck us about our evidence. First, whatever guise evaluation activities went under during the late 1980s and early 1990s, teachers almost always experienced them as 'inspections'. Those who had had experience of one or more alternatives (or thought the issues through at some length) usually had their preferences. But an inspection was still an inspection, whatever it was called. One surprising finding from our own research was that heads and teachers very frequently claimed to have had 'no surprises' when hearing the inspectors' conclusions. If they knew it all already, one might ask, then was the effort really worth it? It took some probing on our part to establish what was *really* new.

So are cheaper approaches on the cards? Costs can usually be reduced by involving schools in more stages of the process and basically getting them to share more of the work. Indeed, many LEAs were adopting less comprehensive alternatives to the OFSTED model for precisely this reason. Schools might, in many cases, have produced something broadly similar themselves. There again, they might have produced something rather different which they felt would be equally useful for their purposes. One of our case studies, however, suggests that in some circumstances they either may not be capable of evaluating themselves, or alternatively may be resistant to doing so (see Chapter 2). This was a school with 'serious weaknesses' which was in danger of 'failing'. The staff in this school were largely unaware, they claimed, of the extent of their difficulties; they were not simply surprised by the inspectors' report but shocked.

Inspection as a basis for school improvement

The crunch question, of course, is whether inspection really does bring about improvement. Regrettably this is a question which it is easier to pose than to answer. And as Perry (1995) reminds us, OFSTED's explicit assertion that it does represent a departure from the previous practice of HMI, although not, it should be said, from that of most LEAs. HMI Frost was not surprisingly committed to the view that it did and, equally importantly, offered some tentative indications of why this might be the case. In his concluding section he stated:

> Reflecting on the first eighteen months of the new inspection system, I am confident that inspection is encouraging schools to focus on their core functions in a systematic way and that through action and development planning schools are gradually improving.
>
> (Frost 1995: 4)

We are inclined to share Frost's optimistic assessment, but there are some problems in doing so. We pointed out earlier that he himself had noted the lack of 'serious mention of inspection' in the literature on school effectiveness and improvement. Self-evidently an inspection is not the only means through which a school can be encouraged to 'focus on its core functions in a systematic way' or to develop plans for action; experience and research indicate that there are other ways (see, for example, Hargreaves and Hopkins 1994). To be truly convincing in this respect one would need to show that the plans of schools which had been recently inspected were of a different order and quality from those produced by schools which had yet to undergo this experience.

In practice the independent evidence on which Frost drew was more limited. A study by Earley and colleagues reported in the *Times Educational Supplement* is the only one cited (Earley *et al*. 1995). This showed that 'the majority of schools had a positive attitude to the process' of being inspected. 'Overall seven per cent of the sample (of 170 schools studied) saw the inspection process as very negative and twenty per cent as very positive in relation to school development.' Inspection, in short, may have got off to a good start. Seeing strengths in the *process* of inspection, however, is not quite the same as showing that it has 'worked'.

Hargreaves (1995) also points to a *lack* of research demonstrating the effectiveness of inspection as a route to school improvement. He suggests, however, that there might be good reasons for this omission. 'The writings of distinguished researchers ... provide little support for mass inspection as a sound strategy, but many reasons why other approaches are to be preferred' (Hargreaves 1995: 119).[13]

We go along with Hargreaves' suggestion that there are 'other approaches' to school improvement (and some of them *may*, indeed, be preferable). Indeed, a short report from OFSTED itself appears to point in similar directions. In a small-scale study of three notably 'improving' schools, produced in 1994, it is suggested that 'to improve anything two conditions are necessary':

> First, we must be very clear about the existing state of things, its strengths and shortcomings. *In this respect the recent introduction of the four-yearly inspection of schools is a very powerful tool.* Next we need a clear vision of what it should look like when the improvement we want has been achieved.
>
> (OFSTED 1994d: 26; our emphasis)

This all sounds very sensible. 'Taking stock' may well provide a good basis for action but there are several ways in which it can be done. The OFSTED study itself scarcely amounted to a ringing endorsement for the 'powerful tool' of inspection. Of the three schools reported on, only one had undergone an inspection in the fairly recent past. In this case the evidence suggested that it was the *stock-taking process* that mattered. Apparently this began around 1989 when the 'needs [of the school] were so pressing that the defects were obvious: poor examination results; poor standards in many subjects; poor attendance; poor morale of pupils and staff . . . ; the budget deficit; and the falling roll' (OFSTED 1994d: 27–8). The school was not, in fact, *inspected* until two years later in 1991.

Another reason why the 'distinguished researchers' Hargreaves mentioned had little or nothing to say about *mass* inspection is, we suspect, rather more mundane. Whilst some would have come across similar sorts of mechanisms, such as 'external review', inspection on the scale experienced in Britain was not merely antithetical to many of their core values but also, quite simply, beyond their experience. There is not much theoretical writing either about the place of inspection in the broader scheme of things (see Chapter 9).

There are further respects in which inspection-led approaches to school improvement have been criticized. Many of the approaches to the evaluation of schools developed by LEA advisers and inspectors paid particular attention to notions of 'partnership' and 'collaboration' (see Gray and Wilcox 1995 for a fuller account). In the run-up to OFSTED this element was initially disparaged and then played down; the roles, it was asserted by some, could not be usefully amalgamated. Inspectors (and those they were working with) should be clear which hat they were wearing. To ignore such relationships may, however, be fatal. As the OECD researchers put it in their report:

> . . . objective external assessment and 'friendly' advice from professionals or peers who know the school well are equally important . . . Simply making schools 'accountable' is unlikely on its own to lead to improvements in performance . . . Care should be taken to build on the expertise and professionalism of teachers and to provide well-focused programmes of staff development which enable them to change, learn to work in teams and to exercise new forms of autonomy fruitfully.
>
> (Brooks and Hirsch 1995: 10)

The implications for current inspection practice, critics suggest, are fairly clear. The limited resources available should be divided more evenly between the two functions.

Our research does not yield simple answers to many of these questions about the effectiveness of inspection as a route to improvement. What we have been able to provide is a fairly sizeable number of cases on which to base the debates (see, in particular, Chapter 7). Furthermore, unlike other studies, we were in a position to follow up what happened in the aftermath of inspection some nine to twelve months later and then again (in the case of the secondary schools in our study) a further six to nine months after that.

In brief, we were in a position to take the longer view. What happened to the best-laid plans? How did schools stop early initiatives faltering? Faced with numerous fronts on which to work, how did schools begin to prioritize? In the event, we were struck by how much the 'outcomes' of inspection, in terms of what got done, varied from school to school. Some simply 'complied' with what the inspectors demanded; others set about the challenges with enthusiasm. Inspection 'works', we concluded, up to a point, but other approaches might have done as well. The real challenge is to identify those contexts and circumstances where it is particularly likely to serve as *the* catalyst.

The 'failing' school: a special case?

One such context may well be that of the so-called 'failing' school. We remember the debates which attended the publication of HMI reports on individual schools in 1983. One of these concerned the Liverpool Institute for Boys, a formerly 'selective' school which had fallen upon harder times. The inspectors were uncompromising in their assessments. Noting the physical decay the school had suffered they described it as 'squalid', the graffiti as 'very offensive' and the toilets as 'insanitary'. 'Overall standards' were 'exceptionally low'. The school was not 'efficiently managed and in some respects it was badly managed'. Whatever the pros and cons regarding publication it is hard to escape the conclusion that something had to be done – and quickly. Liverpool LEA, who were responsible for the school, developed some plans for intervention. After a year or so evidence of improvement was still limited and other plans began to be formulated. Then, some two years after the initial report, it was merged with a neighbouring comprehensive; the school had been re-organized out of existence.

The literature on school effectiveness and school improvement has depressingly little to say about the 'ineffective' school.[14] What is available suggests that such institutions may not know they have problems and/or not be capable of doing much about them without substantial assistance. Those outside who know the school well may be reluctant to act or have difficulty finding a good enough reason for doing so. Inspection, in such circumstances, may provide both the pretext and the opportunity. One such school occurred in the sample of cases we studied and we took good care to ensure that we learnt something of the experience of others (see Chapters 2 and 8). Yet even in these extreme cases it seems that pressure needs to be combined with some support. The school we studied in depth depended heavily on continuing external support to start to pull through and, to some extent, its fortunes waxed and waned according to what was available.

A decade after the debacle of the Liverpool Institute one of OFSTED's first initiatives was to commit itself to dealing decisively with the problem(s) of the 'failing' school. Such institutions would be identified primarily in terms of specified performance criteria and then subjected to so-called 'special measures'. They would be given a short period of time (40 days) to sort out action plans and then be re-inspected about a year later. If they had not made sufficient progress they would be handed over to educational associations who would be free to consider further (potentially drastic) strategies. There was, in short, to be a bottom line.

Assuming for the moment that the performance criteria identified schools which really were 'failing', this 'get tough' policy seems to have worked. It was reported in the summer of 1995 that, faced with such overwhelming pressures for improvement, all but one of the 50 or so primary, secondary and special schools identified as 'failing' had made sufficient progress to avoid this final stage.[15] When schools' futures are really on the line it seems that all but the most embattled can find some seeds of improvement within them.

Our concerns

The impact of inspection on the educational system in Britain promises to be considerable. Its place in the firmament of strategies for holding schools more accountable is relatively well established. Claims about its capacity to initiate or facilitate school improvement, however, are of more recent provenance and need, in our view, to become more firmly based. We know too little about the processes of inspection and its attempts to portray the 'realities' of schools. We need to probe more deeply the ways in which teachers and schools respond to the criticisms inspectors make of them and the challenges which they pose for schools' subsequent development. Crucially, we need to understand more about how best to balance pressure on schools with support for schools when pursuing improvement agendas – not least when schools have 'serious weaknesses' or are in danger of 'failing'.

The chapters which follow attempt to provide some critical perspectives on the rationale(s) for inspection whilst, at the same time, offering a firmer empirical framework within which to locate them. The range of concerns, however, is potentially vast. We hope, at this stage, merely to have laid sufficient foundations for others (and ourselves) to build on.

Our discussion starts with accounts of what happened when the inspectors called on three very different schools.

2 SCHOOLS UNDER THE MICROSCOPE: THREE CASE STUDIES

But optics sharp it needs, I ween
To see what is not to be seen.

(Trumbull, *Canto* i, 67)

School inspection was a relatively infrequent occurrence up to the early 1990s. It would be no exaggeration to say that previously many a teacher would have gone through an entire career without experiencing a major inspection. That will no longer be the case if the arrangements introduced by OFSTED in 1993 continue unchanged into the future. With all schools being inspected once every four years teachers may expect to encounter a school inspection on half a dozen or more different occasions before they retire.

Now that inspections are becoming commonplace there is increased interest in knowing more about them, particularly about their influence on the schools involved. There is still, even now, a dearth of critical accounts either of individual inspections or of the inspection process generally. In this chapter we invite the reader to experience inspection vicariously through the medium of three short case studies. This, it is hoped, will provide something of the feel of an inspection and an initial appreciation of the issues and problems involved. The three inspections considered are drawn from a larger sample of some two dozen.[1] The cases chosen represent both OFSTED and pre-OFSTED forms.

The data from which these case studies have been constructed are derived from interviews conducted with teachers and inspectors on several different occasions following the inspection.[2] In order to preserve the anonymity of those involved, the schools and the LEAs in which they are situated are referred to by fictional names. This device is used throughout the book.

Low Moors Secondary School: a 'good' school's experience of an OFSTED inspection

Low Moors is a large suburban 11–18 secondary school which takes pupils from the full ability range although the distribution is skewed in favour of the more able. About 10 per cent of pupils come from homes where English is not the first language. A similar proportion of pupils are eligible for free school meals.

Low Moors is regarded locally as a 'good school' and this assessment was borne out in its OFSTED inspection report which described it as 'a school with many good features, some of them very good' with many pupils 'achieving levels that are high for their abilities and beyond national expectations'. The quality of the teaching and learning was good and the Registered Inspector (RgI) commented that the number of lessons receiving the highest rating of a '1' was as many as the total the team had awarded in all the schools inspected in the previous year. The management of the school was characterized by 'a clear sense of direction and purpose' with individual departments 'well led with efficient planning processes'.

'The key issues for action' identified a number of areas where further improvement was thought possible, for even a good school can always do better. None of these issues, however, revealed any major dereliction in essential provision. They referred, in the main, to the continuation and extension of initiatives already underway in the school.

Reactions to the findings

The headteacher had generally welcomed the report as fair and one which gave the school the chance 'to reflect and move forward'. As soon as the oral feedback had been received at the end of the inspection week the head quickly set in motion the process for producing the required action plan.

> I would say to any school, as soon as you get that first feedback and you're sure about the key issues, get going on them ... You build yourself up to the OFSTED inspection and then there's a kind of 'whoof' ... you want to keep your momentum going while it's fresh in your mind.

The action plan was completed well within the statutory period and was sent to parents together with the summary of the inspection report. It was anticipated that the majority of key issues would be implemented within the next 12 months.

There were two exceptions to this timescale. The first consisted of a somewhat optimistic recommendation as to future refurbishment: 'when resources are available, continue with the programme of refurbishment of the science laboratories, the gymnasia and hard play areas'. The action plan comment was 'This started in 1989 and will go on for ever!' The second exception drew attention to the need to: 'extend existing arrangements for assemblies to meet the requirements for a daily act of collective worship for all pupils'. This issue is probably more frequently identified than any other in the inspection of secondary schools. It is a particularly intractable problem in large schools like

Low Moors which lack a sufficiently large space to accommodate the full complement of pupils. Although existing arrangements ensured that each pupil had two assemblies a week, the headteacher was at a loss to see how this level of provision could realistically be improved. The action plan expressed a commitment to review arrangements and seek advice from the local adviser for religious education. However, no definite date for implementing the statutory requirement was given.

Of all the key issues the most important for the headteacher was the one concerned with 'establish[ing] monitoring systems to evaluate the implementation of … whole school priorities' involving department and faculty heads. The RgI regarded the failure to have developed such systems as a major weakness of the school, as of others generally:

> the lack of real systematic procedures for finding out whether things were happening at a grass roots level did quite surprise me … A lot was subcontracted to heads of department to manage and most of those heads of department weren't really taking any notice of policies about classroom practice … Schools are essentially so loosely coupled that the only feedback tends to be exam results or performance indicators and an OFSTED inspection, and what they ought to be looking at is building different sorts of feedback mechanisms within school so you really know what's happening.

Was it all worthwhile?

The headteacher, although generally satisfied with the conduct and the outcome of the inspection, did not consider that much of significance had been learned from it: 'I don't think we've learned anything new, I really don't … I mean, I think we could have written the report before they [the inspectors] came. Probably put a lot more into it because we certainly feel we were aware of other developmental points that they hadn't picked up on.'

This assessment may, however, be unduly pessimistic. The RgI commented that initially the headteacher had challenged a key issue which expressed some criticism of the management and evaluation of the school's provision for special educational needs (SEN). The RgI thought that the headteacher had a view about the quality of SEN provision which was not really justified. However, when the RgI presented the evidence the headteacher took it 'on the chin' and accepted that the judgement would appear in the report. If the head was sincerely persuaded that provision was other than originally thought then some new 'learning' might be said to have occurred. The headteacher, however, remained unconvinced that any gains were really worth the 'horrendous' cost in preparing for the inspection and the 'hugely stressful' experience of undergoing it. Similar doubts were expressed by the RgI: 'I think that the other thing that has come out of it is a growing scepticism about whether the whole inspection system at the moment does actually provide value for money. Because I'm not sure that what Low Moors got out of it was worth over £20,000 [the cost of the inspection].'

Doubts about the Framework

The headteacher felt let down by the coverage given to the school's extensive curricular programme. 'We were very disappointed in some subject areas that what had been seen had been ten minutes of one teacher and a quarter of an hour of another and dipping into Year 7 and then rushing off to the sixth form.' A major 'Investors in People' project which involved the whole school – pupils, teaching and non-teaching staff, governors and local industry – had, in the headteacher's view, received only the barest mention in the final report.

Part of the problem here is that the OFSTED Framework sets out exactly what aspects are to be inspected. When the 'specification' for an inspection is negotiated with OFSTED it is up to the school to put forward any additional features which it would like included. The RgI had in fact noticed that the initial specification had omitted any reference to the integrated SEN unit in the school. This was pointed out to the headteacher who contacted OFSTED and, as a result, the specification was modified to include an additional two 'inspector days' to allow inspection of the unit. OFSTED may also, in some cases, include aspects outside the Framework on request provided that the school is willing to fund the additional cost of inspection. In the Low Moors inspection some aspects – including 'Investors in People' – had not been identified by the school and were therefore not included in the final specification. As a result, they only received incidental comment.

Both the headteacher and the RgI thought that the Framework was too restrictive. The RgI particularly regretted the fact that it did not allow inspectors to use any kind of theoretical perspective for interpreting their observations. Although all RgIs are required to comply with the Framework, as the basis for assuring the standard of inspections, it 'is not a theoretical Framework, in fact it is designed not to be – it's designed to stop people using different theoretical perspectives'. This was felt to be unfortunate since such perspectives 'enable you to have more interesting and, I hope, more purposeful dialogue with managers in schools'. The RgI thought that this was not, however, the purpose of inspection as envisaged by the government: 'It's set up to kick shit out of schools. It is set up to identify failing schools and to make it look as if the government has a quality assurance programme for schools ... It isn't really there to fulfil that developmental role with individual schools.'

Murbank Primary School: inspection and the failing school

Growing anxiety

Senior staff of Murbank Primary School were not initially concerned when they learned that they were to be inspected by their local inspectorate. Although aware that 'certain things were not in place', the headteacher's impression of the inspections previously carried out by Falton LEA and known as 'reviews' was that they were supportive and developmental. The deputy headteacher accepted the situation as 'being our turn'. Classroom teachers, however, were rather more anxious and concerned that they might not show their full potential during the inspection.

These initial anxieties were further heightened during the inspection week itself, according to the headteacher: 'Within 40 minutes the feedback from the staff was that all that the inspectors were interested in was criticism – so negative feelings built up by the end of the first day. It wasn't what was expected.' 'As the week proceeded it got worse,' another teacher told us. 'Tuesday was a particularly bad day for the school, people looked stressed – no smiles and children picked up the vibes and began acting silly. It was downhill fast from Tuesday.'

Part of the reason for the staff's reaction was that the inspectors had decided to change their usual approach and to work to the recently published *Framework for the Inspection of Schools* (OFSTED 1992a). This resulted in the inspectors adopting what was perceived as a much more formal way of working, as one teacher put it: 'The inspectors were there, very secretive, concentrating on their business, not able to communicate with them . . . no one put you at ease – they concentrated on the fixed criteria they had to look for.'

The inspectors were aware of the problem and attributed it, in part, to the experience of working to the new Framework which was considered to leave little space for giving feedback during the inspection. The team leader commented: 'My first reaction on coming away from the inspection was "I don't want to be an inspector." Everything previously learned went out of the window and ways of dealing with staff had to take second place.'

Disagreement and trauma

These initial anxieties were, however, as nothing compared to the sense of severe shock which was to follow. The inspectors reported that overall the school was characterized by widespread underachievement and poor curriculum, staff and resource management. Despite the high value placed on the spiritual, social and moral development of the pupils and the good relationships fostered, the school was considered to be failing to provide an acceptable standard of education and was therefore 'at risk'.

The headteacher and staff accepted that some of the criticisms made were justified. Nevertheless, overall the report was considered 'unfair', 'negative', and 'destructive'. Both the headteacher and the deputy headteacher found it difficult to accept that good relationships in a school could coexist with unsatisfactory management and standards of teaching.

The deputy headteacher disagreed with the contention of low educational standards, citing the lack of complaints from the secondary schools to which their pupils subsequently transferred. Furthermore, the school had always received trainee teachers from the local university – this was thought to be surprising if the standards were as reported.

A particular concern about the neglect of context surfaced several times in the comments of both senior staff. 'Context' here referred to the conditions, both in the school and beyond, in which the school's work was conducted.

> The context/background was noted briefly but not taken into account. Most children are from council homes, many are extra-district – many moved to the school by parents who weren't satisfied. The school draws on one of the poorest areas in Falton.
>
> (Deputy headteacher)

The headteacher's concern with context was partly in order to stress factors which helped to explain some of the shortcomings. For example, the lack of a policy in one subject area was attributed to the fact that the schools had been advised not to formulate a policy because the relevant inspector would do so. A policy statement in another subject area was not up to date because of the secondment of the school's coordinator for this subject area. The headteacher's problems with financial planning were the result of not having had, until after the inspection, a secretary competent in the relevant computer skills. Although the report alluded to these points they were probably not seen to be justifiable extenuating circumstances.

The headteacher wondered whether the school's Standard Assessment Task (SAT) scores – which were well below the LEA averages – had coloured the inspectors' perceptions of pupil underachievement. The school had many behaviour and learning problems, the implication being that more account should have been taken of these in judging the school's performance. Moreover, the headteacher had reservations about SATs generally, believing that some schools had 'cheated' in reporting their results.

The inspectors' view of the school was initially presented to the headteacher at an oral feedback on the last day of the inspection week. The headteacher described the experience as feeling 'like being in the dock', 'brutal', and the 'worst that could be remembered'. This was all the more distressing because previously relationships had been on a first-name basis, with inspectors regarded as friends.

The inspectors' comments also had a profound effect on other staff. One commented: 'If this report is true then I should never have been in the job.' Two teachers expressed concern about the possibility of word getting around and affecting career prospects. A particular anxiety was not knowing whose teaching in particular had been considered poor.

The effect of the inspection and its findings was also felt within the inspection team. The team leader referred to the emotional strain building up during the inspection as it became apparent what would have to be said. The team was unprepared for 'the enormity of what was wrong with the school' and the impact on the school staff. Two staff had cried at the feedback session.

In the headteacher's view the experience of the inspection had been 'totally demoralizing ... We actually had a totally happy staff who worked as a team; all this has been pulled from under you and has got to be restored.'

The aftermath: 'heads will roll'

The staff initially found it difficult to accept many of the critical findings. However, they eventually did come to terms with their situation and began to address seriously the problems before them. One prominent influence was the knowledge that there would be a re-inspection of the school a year or so later; this galvanized the staff. As one classroom teacher remarked: 'Governors are very interested in academic achievement and very concerned ... If there is another inspection they will expect a lot will be changed – if not, heads will roll.'

The school inspector also emphasized the interest of the governors in taking action on the recommendations of the report.[3] It was thought that the appointment of a new chairman and two new governors had been influential, resulting in 'searching questions' being asked of the headteacher at meetings.

It was generally agreed that the staff had put in a lot of hard work to tackle the recommendations of the report, particularly during the school holidays. Indeed, one teacher was moved to remark that, as a result, 'professional and family life were all blurring into one. Out of six weeks' holiday I spent two and a half days each week on school work'. The organization of staff meetings had been improved and 'people were working more as a team, sharing more and meeting more regularly'.

It was, however, the school inspector who appeared to have been the crucial factor in the post-inspection phase. The inspector had been able to visit the school regularly and had worked closely with the headteacher and staff, providing ideas and suggestions for tackling the recommendations, at the same time facilitating the involvement of other inspection and advisory staff.

The school inspector was able to continue this involvement for several months; eventually, however, it was necessary to withdraw and to allow the headteacher to manage the school unaided. Regrettably, after withdrawal, things started to go downhill. By the time of the re-inspection, approximately 12 months after the original one, a further critical report was forthcoming. The headteacher retired and an acting headteacher was installed pending a new appointment.

Strafford High School: was it really worth the effort?

At ease with the local inspectorate

Strafford High School is a suburban 11–16 school serving a socially mixed area. It is essentially a community school in all but name. Overall the intake is representative of the full academic range, although there are relatively few pupils of very high ability.

The senior management team of Strafford High School were not unduly worried at the prospect of inspection by the Folkshire inspectorate. They were familiar with the local approach to inspection (termed 'review' in Folkshire parlance). The criteria for inspection had been developed in consultation with teachers and subsequently made available to all schools, which the second deputy headteacher felt was valuable: 'Knowing the Folkshire criteria enables you to manage yourself and know exactly what they will be looking at.' Senior staff were further reassured by the knowledge that the inspection would be led by their school inspector who was well regarded. Some anxiety, however, was experienced by teachers, particularly those who had not previously been inspected.

'I felt some trepidation because I have never been reviewed before although I have been teaching for nine years,' said one head of department. 'Had this image of a horde of grey suited men descending. However, when —— (team leader) visited it all fell into place and the nervousness subsided.' The inspection team leader was particularly concerned that the inspection should go well because the headteacher had a high profile in local teacher politics.

The inspection took place over a week and involved five inspectors. Although the work of all departments was seen the aim was not to report on individual subjects but to focus on whole-school issues. The school's own development plan was used as the starting point and the intention was to assist the process of development and the refining of targets.

An expensive way to get a pat on the back?

On the whole the inspection week went well with the inspectors being regarded as unobtrusive and non-threatening. Some differences were noted between inspectors in terms of the amount of feedback given to teachers after observing lessons. The inspection methods adopted attracted little specific comment apart from some perceived variability in inspectors' approach to interviewing. Inspectors were generally satisfied with their methods although one member felt that some aspects of pupil pursuit[4] could be very time-consuming and not always produce useful information.

The team leader considered that the inspection had confirmed the view that Strafford was a 'good school' which had achieved a great deal in a catchment area that could be problematic. The report was broadly commendatory and well received by the teachers. Although there were 'no major surprises' and 'no new understandings' it was felt that the report confirmed what was already known and that the school was 'on the right track'. The report was widely regarded as having boosted the morale of staff, although as one head of department commented, 'It was an expensive way of getting a pat on the back.'

Another department head opined: 'The inspection felt like a PR job on the school, a PR job from the county, it lacked cutting edge and bite . . . some obvious areas of weakness were not tackled and some areas were beyond the remit of the review.' The first deputy expressed a similar view. 'The report did not have "teeth" sufficient to move us forward . . . the allusions are vague, some departments felt let down because they could not see themselves in the report. The report is too anonymous, it needs to be more specific about where development could take place.'

This concern for more specific detail was echoed by other senior staff:

They were too general in their comments, when they were critical they would not say 'where', 'who', etc because of the anonymity of the process. All it did was to raise questions in our minds and we had to guess which classes were the ones with 'low levels of disruption', they would not give examples . . . they should confidentially inform senior management about specific problems so that they can be improved.

(Second deputy headteacher)

The headteacher and some other senior staff would generally have preferred an approach based on the inspection of distinct subject areas. 'If you do a review you might as well have subject specific inspectors going to specialist subjects,' said the head of IT. 'For example, inspectors are computer literate but they are not IT experts.' At least one inspector had reservations about the general remit of the review:

> I did not feel sufficient history and geography were taught. There was also insufficient time to talk to heads of department to get a full picture of the department – but because there was not a subject brief for the review this information, inadequate though it might be, was not fully utilized. I felt we should have written specific subject reports.

Another had doubts about the overall rigour of the process: 'The Strafford review was fairly untypical, a lightweight review not as gritty and gruelling as some.' Reflecting on the impact of the inspection some six months or so afterwards one head of department commented:

> Was it worthwhile? I am not sure. It produced a bland report which neither offends nor illuminates in real terms. Essentially a question of carrying on the good work and tighten up on some things. We all walked a foot taller when we read the report and it was nice to come out smelling of roses – yes, so perhaps it was worthwhile.

A young classroom teacher appeared more definite: 'The review was not a significant event in my life.'

Some eventual improvement?

Just about a year after the Folkshire inspection the school found itself again the subject of an inspection – this time by HMI under the new OFSTED arrangements.[5] Comparing the reports of the two inspections it is clear that most of the issues raised in the LEA exercise were still there at the time of the HMI inspection. The HMI report, however, was noticeably the harder hitting of the two, particularly in the comments made about the consistency, rigour and challenge of the teaching and learning.

Although the Folkshire review, unlike the HMI inspection, did not report on individual subjects, some indication was given informally of subject areas where lessons were considered favourably. In a few cases the departments well regarded by HMI were not the same as those found by the local inspectors.

> In the case of the LEA review the relationship between the department and the inspector was warmer and more convivial than with HMI . . . The HMI came with his own agenda and stripped us bare and I still haven't recovered. He murdered me – it hurt like hell. However, what he said was true

and fair – but I really felt demoralized. I felt the inspector was deliberately
antagonistic to the LEA review.

(Head of department)

Of the ten recommendations of the LEA inspection report two merely emphasized the importance of continuing with existing initiatives. The remaining
eight, however, were concerned with new developments. A year or so after the
inspection only one of the latter (formulation of an equal opportunities policy)
had been fully implemented although some progress had been made on all but
one of the others. Ten months after the HMI inspection (or nearly two years
after the Folkshire review) a further three recommendations had been at least
substantially implemented. Added impetus had been given to the implementation of two of these (formulation of an assessment policy, more consistent
application of disciplinary procedures) as a result of comments made on these
areas in the HMI report. In addition, work was underway in tackling the key
issue identified in both reports – the development of more challenging and
rigorous approaches to teaching and learning.

Conclusion

Enough has probably been said at this stage to show that inspection is a potentially contentious and problematic activity. A number of key interrelated issues
suggest themselves for more detailed consideration. What is inspection? What
does it claim to accomplish? What does it accomplish in practice? More
specifically, what are the effects of inspection on those inspected and those
inspecting? What effects does inspection have on the functioning of schools?
How and to what extent can inspection result in real change and improvement
in schools? These are issues which lie at the heart of this book. They will be
explored in more detail in the chapters to follow.

3 THE ORIGINS AND
DEVELOPMENT OF
SCHOOL INSPECTION

All changed, changed utterly

(Yeats, *Easter 1916*)

The system of inspection inaugurated by the 1992 Act represents an unprecedented attempt to apply a universal model of inspection of ambitious frequency and comprehensiveness carried out by independent inspectors, drawn from a wide range of backgrounds and operating on a competitive commercial basis. How did all of this come about?

Inspections by HMI (1839–98)

The fortunes of inspection are inextricably bound up with the emergence and development of public elementary education in the 19th century. At the beginning of the century elementary schools were run by voluntary (religious) societies. In 1833 the first government grant in aid (£20,000) was made to the two main societies (the National Society and the British and Foreign Schools Society) concerned with establishing elementary schools.[1] This was at a time when state intervention in education was a highly contentious issue.

After a few years it was apparent that the financial support being provided was insufficient for national needs. If larger subventions were to be made it was necessary to have some mechanism of parliamentary supervision and control. In 1839 the Committee of the Privy Council on Education[2] was therefore established to oversee the allocation of annual grants for promoting public education. Later that year the first two of Her Majesty's (HM) Inspectors were appointed to visit schools.

Lawton and Gordon (1987: 9) suggest that the creation of inspectors for schools was based on the precedent set by inspecting factories, following the Factory Acts in the early years of the century. The benefits of inspection have seldom been more confidently proclaimed than by one witness to the Parliamentary Committee on the State of Education 1834:

> There should be with respect to education a vigilant eye everywhere; and many schools have, for want of that, sunk very materially indeed. Schools cannot be too much inspected and examined ... Such an inspection of all schools throughout the kingdom, I think, would be an unspeakable blessing to society, and would be the means of conveying improvement, and suggesting information to teachers, and stirring them up and leading them to increase their efforts.
>
> (Evidence of Mr W.F. Lloyd, Secretary of the Sunday School Union,
> in Maclure 1969: 33)

In 1840 *Instructions to Inspectors of Schools* were issued which defined the duties of HM Inspectors as: enquiring into applications to build or support schools; inspecting schools already aided by grants; and enquiring into the state of education in particular districts.

Their powers, however, were clearly limited:

> inspection is not intended as a means of control, but of affording assistance ... it is not to be regarded as operating for the restraint of local efforts, but for their encouragement; its chief objects will not be attained without the co-operation of the school committees; – the inspector having no power to interfere, and not being instructed to offer any advice or information excepting where it is invited.
>
> (Minutes of the Committee of Council on Education 1840–1,
> in Maclure 1969: 48–9)

The instructions were also noteworthy for setting out perhaps the earliest expression of what a school inspection might include. This required the inspector to report on: mechanical arrangements (details of the school building and the disposition of desks); means of instruction (the range of subject text books and apparatus); organization and discipline; methods (teaching methods and deployment of staff); and attainments (in different subjects). Particular attention was to be paid to the moral training of the children and, in the case of National Society schools, to determining 'how far the Doctrines and Principles of the Church are instilled in the minds of the Children' (Maclure 1969: 51).

The number of HM inspectors grew over the years and by 1865 there were 67, including assistant inspectors (Lawton and Gordon 1987: 9; 163). At this time inspectors were heavily involved in the direct examining of pupils as a consequence of the *Revised Code* of 1862. This code of regulations instituted a system of 'payment by results' which made a substantial proportion of the grant paid to the managers of schools dependent on pupils' ability to reach certain 'standards' in reading, writing and arithmetic. In 1867 language, geography and history were added as grant-attracting subjects. The implementation of payment by results required even more inspectors and their numbers grew rapidly, reaching 349 at the turn of the century (Lawton and Gordon 1987: 11; 163).

The code was deeply unpopular with teachers and even some HM inspectors. Matthew Arnold, perhaps the most famous inspector, was particularly critical:

> In a country where everyone is prone to rely too much on mechanical processes and too little on intelligence, a change in the Education Department's regulations, which, by making two-thirds of the Government grant depend upon mechanical examination, inevitably gives a mechanical turn to the school teaching, a mechanical turn to the inspection, is and must be trying to the intellectual life of a school . . .
> (from Matthew Arnold's *General Report for the Year 1867,* in Maclure 1969: 82)

The role of the inspector had effectively moved away from that of adviser to that of tester and enforcer of the code (Lawton and Gordon 1987). Although, over the years, the worst features of the code were removed the principle remained in operation until 1898 and persisted as a negative feature in teacher folklore long afterwards.

The emergence of the full inspection

The new century saw the granting of increased freedom to elementary schools and the gradual development of secondary schools as a consequence of the 1902 Education Act. The inspection of secondary schools, with their larger range of subjects and specialist staff, required a somewhat different approach from that adopted in elementary schools, usually involving a day visit by one or sometimes two inspectors. The principal method of secondary inspection was the 'full inspection' which was carried out by a team of inspectors over several days and resulted in a formal report. The justification for such inspections was succinctly expressed by the Board of Education in its *Annual Report for 1922–23.*

> [A] school cannot be judged by a mere review of the subjects taught: it is a living thing: its life, which may have behind it a long tradition, extends beyond the classroom and must be *grasped as a whole*. Periodically, therefore, a comprehensive inspection of the school must be undertaken. The reason why a body of inspectors should undertake such inspection is not so much that the skill of a specialist is needed to inspect specialists, but that *collective judgement on all sides of school life and work is necessary.*
> (Lawton and Gordon 1987: 51–2; our emphasis)

Elementary schools also received 'report visits' at three- to five-yearly intervals although these were not called 'full inspections' until after 1944 (Blackie 1982: 9). During such visits the inspector might examine the children in arithmetic and writing but the practice became less frequent over the years as more reliance was placed on looking at children's work, observing classes and talking to teachers and children.

By 1912 nearly all secondary schools receiving a grant had been fully inspected at least once and most of them twice (Lawton and Gordon 1987: 54). This frequency of inspection was not sustainable and a shortened version of full inspection was introduced in which HM inspectors looked at selected aspects requiring special attention. Full inspections were discontinued during the First World War. Afterwards the backlog of inspections required a change of policy. From 1922 full inspections occurred every ten years instead of five and the number continued to fall.

With the continued growth of secondary schools, the lack of a commensurate increase in inspector numbers and LEA requests for more frequent reports, various alternatives to full inspection were introduced to maximize the use of inspector resources (Lawton and Gordon 1987: 54–6).

The cycle of full inspections continued to decline over the years so that by the late 1950s they had virtually ceased to exist (DES/WO 1982: 11–18). From 1944 onwards, for the best part of 20 or so years, there was a period of broad educational consensus with HMI having largely relinquished its inquisitorial role in favour of a more advisory one. As a result of the low profile of HMI in the 1950s, questions began to be raised about its future and even continued existence. A Parliamentary Select Committee (DES 1968) recommended that full-scale formal inspections should be discontinued, save in exceptional circumstances, and that a greater share of inspection should be left to the inspectorates of local authorities.

By the late 1960s the postwar educational consensus began to fall apart and a series of influential pamphlets – the so-called 'Black Papers' (Cox and Dyson 1969a; 1969b; 1970) – ushered in a period marked by increasing disquiet about the state of public education, by financial crises and cutbacks in education, and by the emergence of educational accountability as a key issue.

In this new climate HMI was able to re-establish a successful national role in which informal visits and full inspections were supplemented by 'short' inspections (dealing with general aspects of schools, not with individual subjects) and national surveys of aspects of educational provision. Surveys often utilized data from questionnaire samples and from full and/or short inspections. The results of surveys of specific phases of education (e.g. DES 1978; 1979) were widely disseminated and were significant influences on the curricular policy and practice of LEAs and schools.

The early eighties was a period where issues concerning the accountability of schools were increasingly debated. The decision in 1983 to publish inspection reports of schools (and colleges) raised the profile of HMI and inspection generally. It also brought their methods and activities more generally into the public arena and provided a foretaste of the influence the publication of reports could have on schools' behaviours and reputations.

The importance of HMI and its inspection activities were unequivocally endorsed by the Rayner Committee (DES/WO 1982). The Committee drew attention to the identity of interest and function of HMI and local inspectorates.

Both services are concerned with assessing standards; with the provision of informed judgements as the basis for policy formation; and with support to teachers through in-service training, curriculum development, and direct advice to individual institutions. The balance of these activities is, however, very different as between the two services.

(DES/WO 1982: 34)

The role of local inspectorates

Local inspectorates had developed in some of the large urban school boards in the late 19th century. They were inherited by the corresponding LEAs which replaced the boards following the 1902 Education Act. Inspector numbers grew slowly in the inter-war years, reaching 500 by 1939. It was not until the curriculum development and school reorganization initiatives of the 1960s and 1970s, however, that their numbers and status increased substantially (Pearce 1986a: 335). The 1974 reorganization of local government, which resulted in the creation of larger and more populous LEAs, provided a further opportunity for expansion. Many LEAs, however, had adopted the alternative titles of 'adviser' and 'advisory services', in place of 'inspector' and 'inspectorates', early signs that the balance of the roles was seen to differ from that of the national inspectors.

The first major research study of LEA advisory services was carried out in the mid-1970s (Bolam *et al.* 1978). When the study was formulated (1972–3) the researchers noted that there was little or no advocacy that advisers should retain, let alone extend, their inspection functions. By the time the research was published (1978), however, the situation had become quite different. This was attributed to successive cutbacks in public expenditure, following the 1973 oil crisis, which led to strong demands for cost-effectiveness and accountability. A second factor was growing public scepticism and debate about education, which had been powerfully expressed in the widely reported speech of the Labour Prime Minister James Callaghan at Ruskin College in 1976. His critical comments about the state of public education initiated a national debate and ushered in an era of curriculum change which was promoted by successive governments over the years.

Into the 1980s: the increasing emphasis on standards

In 1977 LEAs were reminded, in a government consultative document, of the necessity to assess the performance of schools and particularly to identify those which consistently performed poorly (DES 1977: para 3.7). However, rather than an increase in inspection occurring, the trend was towards LEAs encouraging schools to evaluate themselves. A spate of self-evaluation schemes for schools was produced from the late 1970s onwards. Few of these were mandatory, and uptake and commitment varied considerably. The general effect of the initiative was disappointing (Clift *et al.* 1987).

By the mid-1980s concern about the standards of schools, the variability of provision within them, and the importance of local inspection was unambiguously addressed in the Conservative government's White Paper *Better Schools* (DES 1985a). A draft circular followed which encouraged LEAs to review their advisory services and consider how far the various approaches adopted to monitor and evaluate the work of schools should be supplemented by formal inspections (DES 1985b). Although the draft circular was widely discussed, a final version never appeared. A number of LEAs had, nonetheless, developed a strong inspection ethos alongside other approaches. The Inner London Education Authority (ILEA), for example, in the wake of the William Tyndale affair during the 1970s (the name of the primary school which had been pilloried in the press for its poor standards and ideologically motivated teachers), had strengthened its inspection functions but combined these with a more direct interest for school improvement. The innovative Inspectors Based in Schools (IBIS) approach was one expression of this concern to meet the twin needs for accountability and action (Hargreaves 1990). Having identified the fact that a school needed help, the inspection teams then set to work with the schools themselves to initiate remedial action.

Despite the emphasis given to the evaluation and inspection functions of LEAs in successive government and DES reports, there was little evidence of their systematic development in the majority of LEAs. A study carried out in 1986–7 (Stillman 1989; Stillman and Grant 1989) indicated that, on average, advisers spent less than 10 per cent of their time on formal inspections.

A further push towards inspection came with the Education Reform Act (ERA). The ERA represented a powerful expression of the government's commitment to standards, freedom and choice in education (DES 1988b). These implicitly underwrote the importance of evaluation as a means of providing information about schools. In particular, information was needed on how schools were implementing the National Curriculum and the enhanced financial and management responsibilities delegated by their LEAs (both important initiatives of the ERA).

Financial support was made available to LEAs in a five-year programme from 1989–90 to help in the development of coherent inspection policies and in the appointment of extra advisers (DES 1988a; 1989). An influential report on LEA inspectors and advisers was also produced by the Audit Commission (1989). The report was critical of LEAs for having little idea of how inspectors and advisers spent their time. Such evidence as was available, the report suggested, indicated an apparent imbalance between inspection and advice, with far more of the latter than the former.

The report proposed a sophisticated monitoring model involving the systematic recording and analysis of information from three sources: schools (including the results of self-evaluation); inspectors' observations of teaching and learning; the LEA and the DES. Inspectors would systematically record and analyse such information to provide informal feedback to teachers and formal reports to a variety of audiences including the LEA and the governing bodies of schools.

As the 1980s came to an end LEAs were increasingly being urged to develop systems for the effective monitoring and evaluation of school performance. Although full inspections were at least implicitly commended they were seen as one approach amongst a range of possibilities. The phrase which was current at the time was 'inspection in all its forms'. As Kenneth Baker, Secretary of State for Education, put it, knowledge of schools and their teaching 'comes not from educational theories, but from first hand observation – from inspection in all its forms' (Baker 1988).

Inspection and the 'Charter' policy

The end of 1990 saw a change in the leadership of the Conservative Party when Margaret Thatcher was replaced as Prime Minister. In 1991 John Major put forward a Citizen's Charter (Cabinet Office 1991). This set out what every citizen was entitled to expect of the public services: publication of explicit standards; openness and lack of secrecy; availability of full information in plain language; choice wherever practicable; non-discriminatory availability; responsiveness to customer convenience; and the means of redress.

A key role was to be played by inspectorates. They were to provide

> value for money and standards of output and performance. However, their central responsibility is to check that the professional services are delivered in the most effective way possible and genuinely meet the needs of those whom they serve.
> (Cabinet Office 1991: 40)

Changes to inspectorates were necessary, it was argued, if they were not to be 'captured by fashionable theories and lose the independence and objectivity that the public needs'. To this end a number of new measures would be required: lay members would be appointed to more inspectorates; all inspectorates would invite the views of the public; and signed published reports would show the evidence and approach used, and be 'free of jargon'.

In the case of the education service it was asserted that parents needed better information in order to exercise their rights to wider choice of school. A review of HMI was promised which would reflect the need for regular, independent inspection based 'on objective inspection and analysis of performance measures' and carried out by teams which included lay members.

These proposals were duly incorporated in the Parent's Charter launched a few months later by Kenneth Clarke, Secretary of State for Education (DES 1991a; 1991b). He announced the intention of establishing a new organization headed by Her Majesty's Chief Inspector (HMCI) and having fewer HM inspectors. HMI would control the quality of school inspection and monitor the standards of training of the new inspectors. Full-scale inspections would be carried out at least every four years and result in a published report. Parents would be given a variety of pieces of information including a straightforward summary of the inspection report to place alongside performance tables of all schools in the parents' area. 'I intend to take the mystery out of education by providing the real choice which flows from comparative tables setting out the performance of local schools and independent inspection reports on the strengths and weaknesses of each school,' said the Secretary of State (DES 1991b).

Although not stated in the Parent's Charter, the aim was to provide schools with additional funds for inspection. These would be obtained by reducing the revenue support grant to LEAs by an amount corresponding to the proportion of inspector/adviser costs that could be attributed to current inspection activities. Controversially it was proposed that governors of schools would be responsible for making the arrangements for the inspection of their own school. They would be in a position to choose the inspectors they wanted.

In the autumn of 1991 the Education (Schools) Bill was put before Parliament and eventually, in the spring of 1992, became the Education (Schools) Act (DES 1992a). In its fiercely debated passage through both Houses, the Bill received a number of amendments. Perhaps the most significant was the change made to the method for arranging the inspection of individual schools. Responsibility was transferred from the governors to HMCI. In practical terms this meant that arrangements for inspections became one of the principal tasks of OFSTED.

Thus, in the three years or so from 1988, with a new Prime Minister and Secretary of State in post, the government had moved from a position of advocating 'inspection in all its forms' by LEA inspectors to one requiring a universal system of full inspection carried out by independent inspection teams. How is this surprising *volte face* to be explained?

The extent of inspection post-ERA

There is some evidence that the government considered that LEA inspection arrangements were irregular and unsystematic and that this situation was not compensated for by the inspection activity of HMI:

> Previous local authority arrangements in some areas were shameful – irregular and unsystematic visits followed by unpublished reports with little or no evaluation . . . Although there has been some improvement since 1989, it has been too slow and uneven.
>
> (DFE 1992a: 3)

> At the prevailing rate of inspection by Her Majesty's Inspectorate of Schools, before the changes introduced in the Education (Schools) Act 1992, it would have taken some sixty years to cover every secondary school in England, and two hundred years to inspect each of our twenty thousand primary schools.
>
> (DFE 1992a: 8)

No doubt full inspection, long associated with the practice of HMI, was seen as a more systematic and rigorous way to evaluate the performance of schools than those approaches thought to be used by LEAs. It should be noted, however, that full inspection was but one model in the inspection repertoire of HMI themselves (DES 1986).

How had LEAs responded to the evaluation imperative in the period following ERA? Although LEAs claimed to be engaged in a range of inspection and other review activities there was no clear indication of the frequency of inspection (Nebesnuick 1991). We ourselves were able subsequently to remedy this situation by surveying all LEAs in England and Wales (Wilcox *et al.* 1993).[3] Our survey was carried out in early 1992 and asked the chief inspectors of LEAs to give details of their inspection and evaluation arrangements for the previous school year (1990/1).

Our results support the view that in 1990/1 (that is, two years or so after ERA) there had been a significant increase in the amount of school evaluation undertaken in the majority of LEAs. Moreover, there were clear indications that for many LEAs the increase had continued in the following year. In the great majority of LEAs this development had occurred through the adoption of one or other forms of inspection rather than of self-evaluation. Where self-evaluation did occur it was most frequently to be found as an integral part of the annual process of school development planning.

An effect of the 1992 Act and the resulting Framework was to privilege full inspection as the ideal type and a four-year cycle as the optimal rate of inspection. On these criteria the performance of LEAs in 1990/1 appeared modest with only four LEAs carrying out full inspections on 20 per cent or more of their primary schools and only 15 per cent on their secondary schools. However, a further 56 per cent of LEAs conducted full inspections in up to 19 per cent of their primary schools and 34 per cent did so in up to 19 per cent of their secondary schools. In other words, a substantial proportion of LEAs (60 per cent for primary schools; 49 per cent for secondary schools) would have exceeded the 1 per cent figure which Stillman (1989) had estimated as the inspection rate across the country as a whole in the mid-1980s.

Furthermore, when the category of 'part inspection'[4] was included, just over one in five LEAs could then be said to have carried out some form of substantial inspection in at least one-fifth of both their primary and secondary schools. Moreover, if all LEAs were included which conducted substantial inspections in 'some' (i.e. up to 19 per cent) schools the proportion rose to just under 80 per cent. In addition to full and part inspections, many LEAs were involved in one or more alternative types, of which survey inspections and inspections by individual specialist inspectors were the most common.

A main implication of the findings was that the great majority of LEAs could be said to have been following the government's policy of 'inspection in all its forms'. A similar survey of LEAs carried out for 1991/2 (Maychell and Keys 1993) gave results broadly consistent with the general picture we presented.[5]

The political pressure on inspection

Judgements about the prevailing levels of inspection would seem, therefore, to have been unnecessarily pessimistic. The government appears to have been unable or unwilling to recognize the significant change which had occurred in the brief period since the ERA. In the past, the 'evaluation culture' of many LEAs had certainly been weakly developed. Indeed, in some cases, the attitudes in LEAs had been distinctly antipathetic to the notion of the external evaluation of schools. However, the ERA, government exhortations and, to an extent, the specific funding for additional inspector posts and inspector training had combined to change the situation significantly.

Why then did the government not continue to support the development of inspection in LEAs and decide instead to dismantle the existing national and local arrangements? The kind of training programme which was subsequently implemented to establish the new independent inspection teams could arguably have been better targeted at existing LEA inspectorates.

It may be that advice given to government by HMI on this issue had been equivocal if it was in line with the views expressed in HMCI's annual report for 1990/1: 'Just over a third of LEAs had systems in place which inspired confidence in the outcomes of inspection, and just under a third, despite some weaknesses, were improving their capacity to inspect the work in their schools' (DES 1992b: 46). No details were given, however, of the basis on which this remarkably precise assessment was made.

It is more likely that the reasons for the government's actions were dictated by political and ideological reasons. HMI was increasingly subject to hostile comments from Conservative politicians. Bob Dunn, a former junior minister for education, referred to HMI as a 'self-perpetuating oligarchy' who represented the interests of the provider rather than the consumers. He was particularly critical of the 'vague' language of inspection reports and argued that 'consumers want to know which schools are failing and why; they want more precise, statistical information'.[6]

Criticism of HMI was also expressed by others. John Burchill, himself an LEA Chief Inspector, was sceptical about the independence and objectivity of HMI 'apparently torn between the policy of the government and the teaching profession from which inspectors are recruited' (Burchill 1991a: 16). He argued for a new role for HMI on the lines of (or linked to) the Audit Commission, concerned with the licensing and accrediting of local inspectorates. Local inspections would emphasize factual information – for example, examination results and explicit criteria for classroom observation – and produce comprehensible reports. These ideas were subsequently elaborated further in a pamphlet entitled *Inspecting Schools: Breaking the Monopoly* (Burchill, 1991b). This was published by the increasingly influential Centre for Policy Studies, a body concerned with promoting radical Conservative policies.

Concerns about the cutting edge of HMI's monitoring role being blunted by its duality of functions (as public monitors to the system and private advisers to government), and the infrequency of inspections, were also being voiced by the Labour Party (Straw 1991). Labour proposed that HMI should come under the aegis of an independent Education Standards Commission which would be responsible for HMI and coordinate the work of local inspectors.

Many of the criticisms made of HMI were also thought equally applicable to LEA inspectorates. This was particularly apparent in some of the comments made during the tense period when the Bill was being rushed through Parliament just before the forthcoming General Election. For example, junior minister Tim Eggar claimed that Essex, one of the largest LEAs, had only carried out nine inspections since 1944 – an accusation which was subsequently challenged as being completely untrue (Sharp 1992).

Although there was a good measure of agreement between the political parties about the need to reform the current inspection arrangements, there was fundamental disagreement about how this should be done. During the passage of the Bill through Parliament, opposition was vigorously mobilised not only by educationists generally but also by the government's supporters, both in Parliament and in some of the Conservative-controlled LEAs.[7]

Particular pressure was brought to bear on the House of Lords by an influential group which included Sheila Browne, a former HMCI. The Lords subsequently passed two key amendments to the Bill. One, as already noted, removed the proposed right of schools to choose their own inspectors. The other rejected the provision to remove from LEAs the right of entry to inspect their schools. The government, concerned to complete the legislation before Parliament's dissolution for a General Election, accepted both amendments.

Thus the Education (Schools) Act (DES 1992a), although significantly amended in some respects, came to pass and with it a system for organizing inspections, in England at least, which was radically different from that adopted anywhere else. Some understanding of the government's motivations is gained from the following comments of a senior DES official whom we interviewed immediately after the Lords' amendments. On the issue of the intended involvement of governors our interviewee commented:

> the government's stall has been set out very strongly on the basis that governors, including in particular representatives of the community, representing as it were a lay interest in the management of education, are increasingly important . . . [G]iving them additional responsibility is a natural development of that philosophy . . . The link is made that in responding to an inspection report, which is something they would plainly have to do anyway, whoever commissioned it, governors are more likely to take it seriously and be willing to accept that it is important to take action if they have some close involvement in the commissioning process and some choice about, and confidence therefore in, the team carrying out the inspection.

Our interviewee's comments on three other aspects are also revealing. On the primacy given to the full inspection model this person commented:

> I think fairly and simply because government sees this essentially from the perspective of a parent rather than as much from the perspective of the senior management of the school . . . The model which is adopted in those LEAs which do take inspection seriously, in which information is built up about the school cumulatively over a period is, managerially, a perfectly plausible model. What it doesn't do is to give the parent who is, on the whole, interested in the whole school and what it is like as a school – not what the science department was like last year . . . it is a parent-centric operation. That is the distinction the government would make.

On the reasons for extending inspection to private inspectors:

Crudely, a belief in the virtues of competition and in the vices of a monopoly position. Also I suppose, although not an argument which has been advanced quite so emphatically as one might have expected, a belief ... that as the provider of the service, an LEA shouldn't be regarded as the natural source of evidence of how it was doing, how the service was performing, that there was virtue in letting in some independent light ... in ensuring that those providing evidence, if you like, of the quality of education in Barsetshire did not depend on Barsetshire for their own career advancement.

On the problem of ensuring that governors take action following an inspection report:

I don't think it is quite as black and white as you describe it, but at the end of the day, I suppose, one has to admit that the government's general approach is to make the main line of accountability to parents rather than to the LEA: the accountability of the governors to parents as well as of schools to governors. And if you were being unkind you would describe that as a sort of Indian rope trick approach to the quality control of education. But that is the way government is moving inexorably.

These remarks suggest that the Bill was a natural development of previous policy. However, the determination of the government to press ahead with its proposals in the face of widespread opposition may reflect the Prime Minister's concern to set his own distinctive stamp on the Thatcherite legacy he had recently inherited. School inspection and the Parent's Charter were key elements of the Citizen's Charter, his one 'big idea' in the lead-up to the April 1992 General Election. Clearly the proposals could not afford to be lost completely.

Following the Act events moved swiftly: the appointment of a new HMCI; the break-up of the former organisation of HMI; reductions in the number of HM inspectors and the redeployment of others to OFSTED; the training of new independent inspectors; and the development of the Framework and, subsequently, the Handbook. These major changes were successfully completed in time for the first inspections of secondary schools in September 1993 – no mean organizational feat.

Even before the new inspections were underway disillusionment was being expressed by some who had been amongst the most committed to change. John Burchill wrote that 'the monopoly of HMI has actually been strengthened and the best local arrangements are in danger of being dismantled' (Burchill 1993). Sheila Lawlor, influential Deputy Director of the Centre for Policy Studies, considered that 'future inspection will be undermined by virtue of being run by the same people and inspectorates as managed previous LEA and HMI inspection' (Lawlor 1993: 18). She also criticized the Framework for being too detailed, over-prescriptive and having a 'welter of inessential, vague, or woolly requirements, many of which reflect the progressive educational orthodoxies of recent decades' (Lawlor 1993: 11).

Although the target numbers of secondary schools were successfully inspected in the first year of operating the new system (1993/4), there were early indications that the primary programme (which started in September 1994) might not be fulfilled because of the shortage of qualified RgIs tendering for contracts. New recruits were drafted in on a temporary basis.

Summary

We shall leave for the time being the future of OFSTED inspections and summarize some general points which emerge from this review of school inspection. Inspection has, from its beginnings, been part of the broader political context associated with the establishment of a public system of education. The prominence accorded to inspection has varied throughout its history – low in the 1950s and high at the present time. From its origins as single inspectors testing elementary school children, inspection gradually evolved into its most familiar form – the full inspection involving a team of inspectors more concerned with observing a school in operation than in examining pupils directly. The popularity and frequency of full inspections have varied over the years and, at certain periods particularly from the mid-1970s, alternative approaches have been tried. At the present time full inspection has returned to favour in the form of the standardized, universal OFSTED model. As a result more schools than ever before are being inspected.

Although inspection is now being delivered by independent inspectors operating in a competitive market, our principal concerns in this book are with the process of inspection. Our purpose is to assess the practical claims of inspection, provide a conceptual analysis of its practice, and explore its wider educational and social implications.

4   THE CLAIMS FOR

INSPECTION

> They shall give account thereof in the day of judgment.
> (St Matthew 12: 36)

By 1990/1 the majority of LEAs were actively involved in establishing systematic approaches for monitoring and evaluating their schools. Across the country as a whole it could be fairly said that there was a *de facto* programme exploring inspection in its various forms.

The extent of changes which have taken place in LEAs following the Education Reform Act (ERA) is particularly apparent to those familiar with LEAs from pre-ERA days. Undoubtedly, in the past, few LEAs devoted much time to systematic inspection or evaluation. Indeed many inspectors and advisers had had a positive distaste for such approaches and regarded them as irrelevant to their work. The few studies of local advisory services which have been carried out generally confirm our assessment (Bolam *et al*. 1978; Stillman 1989). The government's view of LEA inspection arrangements, contained in the White Paper *Choice and Diversity* (DFE 1992a), was almost certainly based on such earlier assessments. In terms of the post-ERA period, however, it was unduly pessimistic.

We have summarized the major patterns elsewhere in a national survey of all LEAs (see Wilcox *et al*. 1993). By 1990/1 nearly 80 per cent of LEAs estimated that they were devoting a greater amount of inspectors' time to inspection than was the case pre-ERA (over half estimated 'substantially greater'). About 90 per cent of LEAs had programmes of inspection planned ahead for up to a whole year at a time. Formal reports on inspections were made for headteachers and governors in over 90 per cent of LEAs. Although only about one in 20 LEAs made reports available to parents and the press they were seen, in one form or other, by members of the education committee or a specially appointed panel in over 40 per cent of LEAs.

Such programmes were clearly an important outcome of LEAs' response to the educational reforms of the late 1980s. These required the development of more systematic approaches to monitoring and evaluating the implementation of the National Curriculum and the enhanced management responsibilities given to schools. The major architects were LEA inspectors and senior officers. Although just under a fifth of LEAs identified education committee members as influences, they were never the prime movers of the specific evaluation or inspection systems actually adopted. Despite the popular stereotype that 'hard-nosed' inspection was a Tory preoccupation, we found no clear association between the pattern and extent of inspection and the overall political persuasion of LEAs. Commitment to regular inspection was just as likely to be found in Labour-controlled LEAs as in Conservative ones.

In short, a major national experiment had been embarked on in the early 1990s. With the passing of the 1992 Act and the subsequent imposition of the single OFSTED model this was disbanded. What came into being was essentially the traditional 'full' inspection as practised by HMI in the 1980s. It is to a brief consideration of the major features of this model that we now turn. How was it supposed to work?

The full inspection

In a 'full' inspection a team of inspectors was led by a 'reporting' inspector (RI) who was responsible for the inspection as a whole.[1] The number of inspectors in the team varied according to the type and size of the school.

The inspection process fell into three phases. In the pre-inspection phase the RI visited the school to inform the headteacher and staff about the forthcoming inspection and to make the necessary arrangements (including the collection of documentation for the team to study prior to the inspection).

During the inspection phase, which typically lasted for up to a week, inspectors spent as much time as possible observing the work of pupils in classrooms and elsewhere. In addition they talked to pupils and staff, looked at samples of pupils' work and attended other activities such as assemblies, registration and tutorial sessions, as well as a selection of extra-curricular activities. Towards the end of the inspection the findings were presented orally to the headteacher and other senior staff. The school was encouraged, at this stage, to identify any factual inaccuracies or interpretations which were considered ill-founded. The RI would then go away and draft a report.

In the post-inspection phase a meeting with the governing body was convened to hear and comment on the main findings before the report was published. The report appeared, if possible, within six months of the inspection. The contents of reports were organized under a common set of general headings. In the case of maintained schools, copies of the report were sent to the chief education officer of the LEA, the clerk to the governors and the headteacher. Fourteen days later the report was published and became freely available. LEAs were required to indicate, within four months, what action was to be taken in the light of the report's findings. The amount of 'action' deemed necessary varied, of course, from school to school.

What's different about OFSTED?

The 1992 Act changed the arrangements for inspection in several fundamental ways. First, it inaugurated a four-year cycle of inspection which involves a volume of inspections being carried out on a national scale far greater than that achieved previously – certainly in this country and probably anywhere else.

Second, it has opened up inspector recruitment to a wider range of people than ever before. Apart from the earliest days,[2] school inspectorates (both national and local) have recruited their members almost exclusively from the teaching profession. A key qualification for selection has always been that of professional excellence. Applicants who now wish to become inspectors are not necessarily debarred because of lack of teaching experience, although they do have to indicate which phase (primary, secondary or special) they wish to operate in and the subject/aspects they could inspect. The recruitment base for OFSTED inspectors has been further broadened to allow the appointment of 'lay' inspectors, one of whom has to be included in each inspection team. The key requirement for lay inspectors is that they are *not* educational professionals.[3]

Third, the right to carry out inspections has been invested in a cadre of *independent* registered inspectors who are responsible for assembling teams of inspectors. Independence is further sought by the requirement that an inspection team must not include inspectors previously involved in the work of the school concerned (for example, through providing advice and support).[4] In practice many inspections have been carried out by teams employed by LEAs.[5] If inspectors are independent of the school it is assumed that they are impartial in their judgements. This was a factor which helped to ensure the credibility of HMI in the past; HM inspectors had no personal stake in the schools they inspected and so were not beholden to those responsible for their management. The issue of independence is central to OFSTED arrangements and is further embodied in the fourth fundamental characteristic. This requires that contracts for the inspection of any school be open to all RgIs who wish to bid under conditions of competitive tendering.

Fifth, the arrangements require a much speedier reporting and clearer follow-up process (to include parents) than was the case with HMI in the past. A report to the school governors together with a summary for parents now has to be produced within 25 working days of the end of the inspection. Governing bodies, in turn, are required to produce action plans within 40 days setting out procedures for implementing the key inspection findings. Copies of action plans are to be sent to parents within a further five days (DFE 1993a).

Sixth, guidance for carrying out inspections is provided in the Framework which is, in turn, a key section of the more detailed Handbook. While HMI previously had a document outlining its approach to inspection (HMI 1988a) it was purely for internal use and was not available to outsiders. By contrast the Handbook has no such restriction and can be purchased by anyone. The Handbook is also much more extensive and elaborate than its HMI predecessor.

Finally, special attention is given to 'failing schools'. Such schools may be taken over by an 'education association'[6] if the Secretary of State considers that 'the school's action plan or the local education authority's proposals for action are inadequate, [or] where he [*sic*] is not convinced of their ability to implement their plans effectively or where action goes ahead as set out in the plan, but monitoring shows it is inadequate or is not being implemented effectively' (DFE 1993a: Appendix A).

The inspection process

The inspection process as set out in the OFSTED Handbook was devised by HMI in the relatively short period of time between the passing of the 1992 Education (Schools) Act (March 1992) and the start of the training courses for the new independent inspectors (September 1992). The model had to reflect the requirements of Section 9 of the Act which defined the functions of inspection as reporting on:

1 the quality of education provided by the school;
2 the educational standards achieved in the school;
3 whether the financial resources made available to the school are managed efficiently; and
4 the spiritual, moral, social and cultural development of pupils at the school.

These four elements are clearly visible in the main headings which structure an OFSTED inspection report:

1 *Introduction*
   Basic information about the school, intake of pupils and areas served, school data and indicators.
2 *Main findings and key issues for action*
3 *Standards and quality*
   Standards of achievement, quality of learning.
4 *Efficiency of the school*
5 *Pupils' personal development and behaviour*
   Spiritual, moral, social, cultural development, attendance.
6 *Subjects of the curriculum and other curricular provision*
7 *Factors contributing to these findings*
   quality of teaching
   assessment, recording and reporting
   quality and range of the curriculum
   equality of opportunity
   provision for SEN
   management and administration
   teaching and non-teaching staff
   resources for learning

accommodation
pupils' welfare and guidance
links with parents
agencies and other institutions.

(adapted from OFSTED 1994b: (2) 17–36)[7]

'Standards' are defined as 'standards of achievement' and 'quality' as 'quality of learning' and 'quality of teaching'. The first two of these form the main section 'standards and quality' while the latter is included under the heading 'factors contributing to these findings'. The other two requirements of the Act appear as 'efficiency of the school' and 'pupils' personal development and behaviour'.

The remaining main headings are very similar to those employed in the past by HMI in the inspection reports of *secondary* schools:

1 *Introduction*
Information and statistics on the school and its catchment.
2 *Quality of pupils' work*
Climate and attitudes, standards of work, support for learning.
3 *Provision*
Premises, equipment and resources, library and media resources.
4 *Staffing and management*
Staff, management, staff development.
5 *Curriculum and organization*
General, Years 1–5, sixth form.
6 *Assessment and recording of progress*
7 *The school community*
Pastoral care, guidance and counselling. The school as a community. The school in the community.
8 *Conclusions*
9 *Subjects, courses and aspects of the curriculum*
10 *Appendices*
Staff development, curriculum analysis, exam results, attendance figures.

(adapted from HMI 1988a: part 2)

The sections in the HMI model (1988a) on 'quality of pupils' work', 'subjects, courses and aspects of the curriculum' and 'conclusion' appear as the OFSTED report headings 'standards and quality', 'subjects of the curriculum and other curricular provision' and 'main findings and key issues for action'. Sections 2 to 7 of the former HMI reports are effectively reconstituted under the heading 'factors contributing to these findings' in the OFSTED variant. The 'introduction' section common to both incorporates in the new version *inter alia* much of the statistical information that would formerly have been included as 'appendices'. An OFSTED inspection is therefore a kind of hybrid based on the specific requirements of the 1992 Act and HMI's former approach to secondary inspection. It is, however, much more comprehensive in its coverage and should, perhaps, be regarded as a 'very full' full inspection.

Other features of the content of the Handbook may be regarded as more detailed, explicit and elaborated versions of those to be found in the previous

HMI document. For example, some indication had previously been given of what features to look for under the various aspects of the school. In the Handbook these are developed into detailed lists of *evaluation criteria*. Further guidance is given in Part 4 of the Handbook where the criteria for each aspect are amplified by the provision of contrasting paragraphs, one describing a 'good' situation and the other an 'unsatisfactory' one. Furthermore, guidance is offered on the issues to be considered when reviewing evidence and what should be taken into account when reaching a judgement.

Inspectors are required to rate various aspects (such as standards of achievement; quality of learning; and quality of teaching) on a five-point grading scale. These gradings can be aggregated and together with ratings of other aspects of the school (using seven-point scales) form a major part of the Record of Inspection Evidence (RoIE). This Record serves two main purposes: to organize key evidence in a form which assists the inspection team in making clear judgements; and to provide HMCI with a formal return of the evidence on which the inspection findings are based. The origins of this part of the OFSTED methodology can be found in the use of grading scales by HMI in the past (HMI 1988b).

The range of inspection evidence on which judgements are made is similar to that previously employed by HMI (and LEA inspectorates). There are, however, some significant additions. For example, parents' views on the school are to be heard at a specially convened meeting. In addition, if the governors agree, parents may be invited to complete a standard questionnaire giving their views on the school. The range of pre-inspection documentation that a school is to provide is specified in detail and the headteacher completes a comprehensive questionnaire dealing with the organization of the school. The latter requires *inter alia* the provision of a variety of statistical information.

Inspections are usually carried out within the period of a week and the general organization follows the normal three stages of pre-inspection, inspection, and post-inspection. What the Handbook essentially does is to set out in explicit detail what each of the stages involves and the procedures necessary to carry them through.

In essence, then, OFSTED inspection can be considered a 'mutation' of HMI's former approach to secondary inspection. It is a mutation more elaborated than its parent and one where, to pursue the biological metaphor, the 'phenotype' is specified in the form of explicit guidance, procedures and criteria in the Handbook – the inspection 'book of life'.

Views of Chief Inspectors on the OFSTED approach

Different LEAs had been developing different approaches to the monitoring and evaluation of schools. We asked our panel of Chief Inspectors (CIs), which was drawn randomly from one in five LEAs in England and Wales, for their reactions (see Wilcox and Gray 1995 for further details).

All regarded the Handbook as 'useful' although overall views of it ranged from the enthusiastic to the lukewarm. 'The OFSTED Framework and Handbook is an excellent tool. If we had had this in 1988 we would have been in a different position. It is a real treasure' (CI, Weldon). 'Anything which lets the dog see the rabbit is useful – in that sense the Framework is useful' (CI, Sedley). Although the OFSTED approach was generally commended for its thoroughness, explicit detail and comprehensiveness, some inspectors foresaw its potential for bureaucratic inflexibility. The understandable desire of the Handbook's authors to achieve standardization and an 'inspector-proof' model has to be balanced against the dangers of creating a prescriptive and unwieldy leviathan.

> A mind-blowingly large volume of evidence is required. The Framework is potentially helpful – I haven't found a school yet that didn't feel the Framework wasn't helpful. However, at the same time, the degree of information required runs the risk of overwhelming the process itself.
>
> (CI, Hartshire)

The most frequently cited reservations were concerned with what may be termed the 'logistics' of inspection. These included: the costs; the number of inspectors required; the time demands made on inspectors; the contract bid system; and the feasibility of maintaining a four-year inspection cycle. There were also doubts about the availability of a sufficient pool of experienced inspectors, particularly in the primary field.

Anxiety was also apparent in comments made about post-inspection activities, notably the provision of subsequent support and advice.

> Once the inspection is over the school needs support to move forward but there is an ambiguity about whether you can go back and give advice. In many ways the best person for further advice is the inspector – rather than someone coming in 'cold' from outside. We feel that in inspections we could say much more than we are allowed to. Governing bodies need to be able to contact someone to come in and interpret the report.
>
> (CI, Foxton)

Such anxieties were also reflected, to some degree, in a review of the first hundred secondary OFSTED inspections carried out on behalf of OFSTED by the management consultants Coopers and Lybrand (OFSTED 1994c). It is evident that Chief Inspectors adapted rapidly to the new demands brought about by OFSTED's establishment. It is notable, however, that many were aware of the break this represented with their own previous practices. What would have emerged if their own 'experiments' had been allowed to run their course? Our research suggests that whilst there were some differences there were some continuities as well. It is to some of this evidence that we now turn.

Alternatives to 'full' inspection

The volume of full inspections (or 'reviews' as they were often called) was undoubtedly low in the majority of LEAs. However, as already noted, when the various forms of 'part' inspection were included a substantially higher level of school inspection was revealed.[8] Indeed if other types of inspection had been taken into account the extent of schools' involvement in 'inspection in all its forms' would have been even greater. Two further types were also popular. In the 'theme' or 'survey' inspection a single report was produced on one or more aspects across a number of schools. Such inspections were used in about three quarters of all LEAs in 1990/1. 'Specialist' inspections, where a report on a specific aspect of a school is produced (often involving a single curriculum area and inspector) were found in over half of all LEAs.

'Self-evaluation' is an alternative to inspection. This is where teachers carry out an evaluation of their own school or aspects of it. Although some LEAs in the late 1970s and early 1980s had developed schemes of school self-evaluation (Clift *et al.* 1987), these were little in evidence by 1990/1.

So what decisions had individual LEAs taken about the forms inspection would take? The first point to be made is that they had almost all opted for inspection in one or more of its various forms. Of the 22 LEAs in our panel 20 had gone this way. Only two could be described as being traditional 'pre-ERA' advisory services, having no regular programme of systematic school inspection. In one of these LEAs the CI reported that the Chief Education Officer (CEO) had pronounced that 'schools in North Mallingham will be inspected over my dead body'.[9]

In the majority of those LEAs going down the inspection route, developments had clearly been prompted by the ERA and the new appointments of Chief Inspectors and CEOs which often followed. In two LEAs, however, education committee members had exerted pressure for a more explicit approach to the monitoring and evaluation of schools.

About two thirds of LEAs were committed to implementing regular school inspections (on cycles ranging from four to ten years) which, although generally less comprehensive than traditional full inspections, were concerned with whole school issues. These were known by a variety of names – 'performance reviews', 'team inspections', 'whole-school reviews' – and corresponded to the 'full and/or part' designation used earlier. CIs tended to be doubtful of the value of full inspections particularly for secondary schools where alternatives were preferred:

> I'm very sceptical about the efficacy of full inspections at secondary level in that I feel that they are going to have insufficient detailed comment to enable schools to effect improvement . . . The headteachers and governors have said, and it's a view we agree with, the most effective type of inspection for them is the 'departmental inspection' because they do get in-depth reporting on a particular curriculum area.
>
> (CI, Queensbridge)

The majority of LEAs had developed monitoring programmes consisting of from two to four different inspection types; Southcastle, however, had an extensive repertoire of six. Apart from variations on the full, part, specialist and survey types identified in our larger LEA survey, three further forms are worthy of comment.

The first, represented by just under a quarter of LEAs, was variously termed 'consultative', 'negotiated' or 'contract' inspection. In these the initiative for inspection came from an individual school with whom the inspectorate negotiated an agreed contract. Such inspections had been introduced in

1989/90 by, for example, Weldon LEA. The CI explained the advantages in the following terms:

> Right from the start we have presented our activities as a partnership with schools and that our respective responsibilities are towards improving provision for young people ... Now we felt obviously that it was important ... if it is a partnership ... there ought to be ways in which schools were encouraged honestly and openly to say 'This is an area where we're not sure of the level of our provision, we're not sure whether we're giving the kids a good deal. Can you come in and work with us on that?' ... Because the report is not published it does mean that there is a degree of openness and honesty ... and we've tried very hard to keep those reports confidential to the school and to the governors so that they don't go to committee, and ... members are content with that.

The second variant was employed in nearly half the LEAs and involved individual inspectors making visits to schools (usually for a day). The extent to which such visits were programmed in advance and resulted in formal reports varied. The Southshire CI argued that such visits represented a more efficient use of inspectors' time than full inspections:

> We're at the 'critical friend' end of the discussion and the view we take is that the most efficient use of an inspector's time generally would be to visit as a singleton, to make sure that classroom observation took place and to make sure that an oral report is given at the end of the visit which is then followed up by a 'note of visit' ... in the year in question [1990/1] we visited and produced notes of visit on about 6000 occasions. That works out at an average of four to five to each primary school and up to 25 visits to a secondary school, and those would be visits by both specialist inspectors and by the phase [school] inspector.

The Vertsey inspectorate was developing a modification in which notes of visit for each school built up over a four-year period into a portfolio of data. This then led to a review conducted by a small team of inspectors in the fourth year.

Sedley was one of the two LEAs in our interview sample which had adopted an inspector-validated or supported self-evaluation system. In the Sedley variant the intention was that every school would engage in two major evaluations each year so that over a five-year period all the main areas of a school would be covered. One or two staff planned and carried out the evaluation against a set of agreed criteria and wrote a report. Meanwhile an inspector conducted a sample evaluation, usually over two days, and wrote a commentary to supplement and validate the school's own report. A modification allowed the report to be written jointly by the inspector and school staff after consultation to agree the contents.

The Sedley CI was cautious in assessing the effectiveness of the approach:

> Validated self-evaluation is a wonderful system for a healthy school ... It has got considerable problems in a school that isn't ... it doesn't work unless there is an enormous input to make it work and the baseline for

that input is very probably not there, and the only way you could get the baseline for that kind of input would be . . . an inspection.

Apart from the decision to opt for a wider variety of approaches to inspection there was another dimension in which LEAs had developed alternatives to the OFSTED approach. This was in the extent to which they made deliberate efforts to *involve* those being inspected in the inspection process.

Just over a quarter of LEAs in our survey (Table 4.1) claimed that their schools had considerable involvement in determining what was to be inspected. A similar proportion involved schools in the collection of data although this was largely confined to bringing together relevant school documentation and statistics. In a minority of LEAs school staff also participated in determining how to inspect, analysing inspection data and deciding the content and recommendations of inspection reports.

Notwithstanding the differences of emphasis within different LEAs, to all intents and purposes we can regard inspection as a generic title for all of those activities in which the evaluation tasks are predominantly carried out by inspectors. We shall generally refer hereafter to 'inspection', 'inspectorates', and 'inspectors' even where alternatives such as 'review', 'advisory services', and 'adviser' were used in some LEAs.

Improvement, accountability and standards

The essential purposes of inspection, apparent from its early days, were succinctly expressed by the Weldon CI:

> HMI have always . . . been seen as having primary responsibility to report the conditions of schools to the Secretary of State. Now that has clearly been one of their most important responsibilities, and I recognize that, but as a secondary responsibility . . . and very much the philosophy of the inspectorate, there has been the idea which they sometimes rather cryptically put as 'doing good as you go' . . . The opportunity . . . [for this] is much greater in an LEA simply because the prevalence of contact is greater than it can be in any HMI or privatized system of inspection, simply because you are there all the time.

Table 4.1 Involvement by LEA of school staff in inspection activities

Aspect of inspection	degree of involvement			
	none/ minimal	some	considerable	not answered
What to be inspected	28	41	27	4
How to be inspected	54	34	7	5
Collecting data	19	53	24	4
Analysing data	75	13	4	8
Content and recommendations of report	52	32	11	5

Source: Questionnaire to all English and Welsh LEAs (n = 100)

In other words, inspection is concerned both with accountability (reporting to those to whom a school is accountable) and the improvement of schools. For the Weldon CI the latter was the prime function, particularly for an LEA inspectorate.

Although not expressed so explicitly, the views of other CIs also tended to reflect an 'improvement' rather than an 'accountability' rationale. It was only the Rodley CI who put the emphasis more on the accountability function:

> The inspections here are principally telling the council members how well the schools are doing. That's the main agenda and we are there because obviously they rely on us to tell them from our evidence what they perhaps ought to have as priorities, what questions they ought to be asking.

The reporting procedure adopted by Rodley was consistent with this emphasis on accountability. Reports of inspections were presented to a panel of councillors with the headteacher and chair of governors of the school concerned in attendance.

The notion of improving schools is closely related to that of 'raising standards' – a slogan that has dominated much of the educational debate in recent years. The acid test of the improvement thesis of inspection is that the standard of pupils' learning, measured usually as performance on tests or examinations, is raised.

Chief Inspectors were able to describe examples where they felt that improvement had resulted from an inspection; however, none was able to cite strong evidence for enhanced pupil performance. Convincing demonstration of the latter would be difficult and require a long-term follow-up of pupils. Improvements where cited, therefore, were invariably described in terms of such features as management, classroom organization, teaching and the like. In other words, improvement was interpreted as raising standards of *process* (broadly conceived) rather than *performance*. The assumption is, of course, that improvements in process lead to improvements in performance.

Two inspectorates (Folkshire and Sedley), in common with some others elsewhere, had sought to make especially explicit the process standards by which their inspections would be guided. Typically, standards were expressed as hierarchical lists of 'criteria'. For example, Folkshire's criteria were organized under five broad headings describing what were seen as the main organizing features of a school: aims; ethos; curriculum organization and assessment; curriculum implementation; and management and administration. Each of these in turn were divided and subdivided into more detailed statements. The criteria had been published as a booklet and widely circulated to schools. Folkshire's Chief Inspector explained the rationale of the booklet:

> We manage to avoid ideological statements ... we're really concerned there with a document based on 'effective schools' research and those are generic criteria for reviewing whole schools but many specialist advisers working with their heads of department have produced subject-specific ones that are based on them.

The concern for 'ideology-free' criteria was also claimed by some other CIs, particularly when making judgements about teaching:

> If, in the classroom, the teacher's standing at the front, his blackboard covered in work, all the pupils have got their heads down copying from the blackboard, then if the teacher says to me, 'I am doing this as a control mechanism because of this, that and the other,' that I will accept. As long as there is a very good reason for it and it has been thought through.
>
> (CI, Stockpool)

Rodley's CI also felt strongly about avoiding dogma and argued that inspections should be based on 'facts'.

> I am concerned that people don't peddle their own views – making dogmatic assertions that classrooms must conform to certain characteristics ... Assertions must be supported by facts. For example, criticisms of children's behaviour would need to be substantiated by such information as 'amount of time lost'.

Performance standards, usually in the form of examination and test results, were, however, often included in inspection reports to help set the context of the school and/or provide an indication of pupil achievements.

We asked CIs how their LEAs had attempted to raise educational standards generally. In a few LEAs particular emphasis had been given to raising standards in the 'basics'. In the majority, however, the improvement of standards was conceived much more broadly and embodied in a range of initiatives. These latter included: the LEAs' in-service programmes for teachers in such areas as the implementation of the National Curriculum; school development planning; and teaching and learning approaches. Involvement in a variety of local and national projects was also seen as contributing to raising standards.

By the time of our third and final interviews, carried out in 1993/4, increased interest was being shown in more quantitative expressions of standards. LEAs had clearly taken seriously the government's commitment to 'league tables' and were engaged in various attempts to develop 'value added' analyses, in a couple of cases in conjunction with external research projects. Inspection was usually included as one among a range of initiatives premised on the notion of improving schools, although it was not necessarily regarded as the most important. The CI for Greenshire attempted to assess the impact of what were considered the three major initiatives in the LEA for raising standards: 'Teacher appraisal is potentially the most valuable, then school development planning, and then inspection. If value for money is the criterion then school development planning should come further up the hierarchy.'

On the whole, CIs were cautious in making generalised claims for the efficacy of inspection. Where improvement was considered to have arisen as a consequence of inspection[10] two factors were frequently cited, 'partnership and collaboration' and 'support and follow-up' (see Gray and Wilcox 1995).

'Partnership and collaboration' could refer to the way in which an LEA had involved its schools in the development of its general inspection policy and procedures. The term could also characterize the relationship between inspectors and school staff during an actual inspection. Considerable attention had been paid to developing mutual trust and respect between inspectors and school staff. Major emphasis was given 'to support as opposed to accountability' in order 'to prepare a school to look at a focus causing concern' or to help a staff 'accept the credibility of the findings'. 'Honesty and openness' were perceived as central ingredients in this process. LEA teams had had to work hard to get themselves perceived as 'supportive and helpful'. The nurturing of 'staff involvement' was seen as a guiding principle in these activities.

Aspects of 'support and follow-up' were mentioned by about half the CIs. This particularly included the formal and targeted provision of in-service activities and the making available of advisory teacher support.[11] The importance of informal but intensive work with headteachers and advisory staff was also mentioned. Rodley LEA reported having developed a system of 'minders' which involved a heavier inspector presence after an inspection had shown a school to be in particular difficulty.

Follow-up also took place in a number of other ways. There was formal monitoring of progress after inspection, including the setting of targets. Sometimes schools were given extra resources to encourage post-inspection development. A few LEAs also reported having procedures for longer-term follow-ups as much as 12 months later.

Conclusion

What we have essentially suggested in this chapter is that despite their different titles ('specialist', 'part', 'full', 'OFSTED') all the activities so described share sufficient similarities to justify the common label 'inspection'. While there may be no one single feature that is common to all inspections – as we have seen, even the roles of 'inspector' and 'inspected' are not absolutely distinct – nevertheless certain 'family resemblances' are apparent. Inspections constitute a 'family' of broadly similar activities.[12]

So far our emphasis has been on describing the external features of inspection – its alleged purposes, organizational structures and methods – from the viewpoint of inspectors. It is now time to turn to a detailed look at the internal processes of inspection and the effects that inspection has on those involved. In doing so, we shall evoke the voice of the 'inspected' no less than that of the 'inspectors'.

5 THE EXPERIENCE OF INSPECTION: PRESSURES AND ANXIETIES

> I don't like the business any better than you do. But, you
> know, I had a premonition of it. I was dreaming all last
> night about two enormous rats! Upon my soul, I never
> saw such brutes, huge black ones! They came, sniffed,
> and went away again!
>
> (Gogol, *The Government Inspector*)

It may come as something of a surprise to learn that there has been little serious research into the effects of school inspection. Although over the years periodic doubts have been raised about its value these have traditionally been resolved by the deliberations of consultative committees or enquiries (see, for example, DES/WO 1982) rather than of researchers. Accounts of individual HMI inspections have also occasionally been written up in the educational press by the headteachers or teachers who experienced them (Barnes 1983; 1984). Some more extended accounts have appeared as student theses in postgraduate courses in education (see Miles 1982). More recently further examples of these kinds of account have emerged, initially with the growth of LEA inspection and then with the introduction of OFSTED inspections.[1] Despite these individual efforts, inspection remains under-researched and, partly as a consequence, under-theorized. The situation is, however, changing, as OFSTED inspections become an interest of academic researchers (see, for example, Brimblecombe *et al.* 1995a; Ouston *et al.* 1996).

In our own research[2] we have sought to provide a critical appraisal of the inspection process and its effects by focusing on individual cases. We draw on this research here and in the chapters which follow.

Case studies of inspection

Our cases consist of 24 inspections of both primary and secondary schools in several LEAs. The LEAs were chosen originally to explore the effects of different approaches to the inspection and evaluation of schools. Our aim was to study two primary and two secondary school inspections in each of six contrasting LEAs. Mortdale and Churdley were chosen as examples of LEAs which until recently had little tradition of systematic inspection but had quickly implemented inspection programmes in the last couple of years. By contrast, Forestshire maintained a well-organized and established inspection programme extending back to the 1970s which had continued to evolve over time. Falton and Folkshire provided examples of somewhat different approaches to whole-school inspection or 'review' as it was more generally termed.

Sedley was one of a small number of LEAs which had continued a commitment to school self-evaluation. At the time of its selection it was involved in a form of inspector-supported self-evaluation. In Sedley we were restricted to the study of three rather than four cases.[3] A single inspection from Middleshire was also included because the LEA had experience of lay inspector involvement and the use of a parents' meeting and questionnaire in its own approach to inspection – all before these became features of OFSTED inspections.

The passing of the 1992 Education (Schools) Act (DES 1992a) in the early months of the study had an inevitable effect on our LEAs and their approaches to inspection. This was because they began to adjust their existing arrangements to conform to the full inspection model which would become the norm in 1993 and 1994. If the LEAs were to compete successfully for future inspection contracts they had to build up experience of the 'new' approach. As a result, the inspections which we negotiated to study over the period 1992–4 included a mix of the relatively unmodified inspections and others carried out in late 1992 or early 1993 based on the OFSTED Framework and Handbook (see the Appendix for details). With the benefit of hindsight it is clear that this was an important transitional period. The experiment of 'inspection in all its forms' was sufficiently well-established for participants to have formed views about the strengths and weaknesses of the various kinds of inspection they had experienced. They used this knowledge to inform their critiques of the OFSTED-related developments in which many of them were becoming involved. They brought a freshness of perspective and a critical edge to their initial encounters with the OFSTED approach which partly resulted from their view that it represented just one alternative. Subsequently we noted that some of their criticisms became more muted as the OFSTED approach became the norm.

The range of inspection types covered included part inspections (which incorporated the Sedley supported self-evaluations), full inspections, and OFSTED inspections. Those classified as 'full' were not as comprehensive as the OFSTED inspections and did not necessarily include *inter alia* detailed reports on all curriculum subject areas. They may be regarded as 'whole-school' inspections to distinguish them from the part inspections. The dividing line between the two categories is, however, to some extent arbitrary.

Each inspection was studied using individual, semi-structured interviews with small samples of teachers and inspectors.[4] The aim, in essence, was to elicit individual reactions to the inspection process as soon after inspection as possible and when teachers knew of the general findings. Follow-up interviews were also carried out later to explore the effects of the inspection on the school's subsequent development.[5] In addition, interviews were supplemented, where possible, by opportunities to observe the planning and the conduct of pre- and post-inspection activities.

Our aim here is not to provide detailed accounts of individual inspections but rather to identify the range of issues and concerns which arose when schools underwent both OFSTED-style and pre-OFSTED inspections. We subsequently extended the range of cases by interviewing headteachers and inspectors involved in five more recent OFSTED inspections in two further LEAs (Besford and Loamshire). This was to provide some indication of the extent to which issues and concerns identified in the earlier inspections had persisted in later ones. Our general view was that the parallels were more striking than the differences.

Reactions to the prospect of inspection

Reactions to the prospect of being inspected varied according to where one was in the school hierarchy. Headteachers and their deputies generally accepted the prospect of being inspected without particular trepidation and in some cases positively welcomed it.

> My immediate response to the invitation to participate [in a 'pilot' OFSTED inspection] was 'yes'. It was an opportunity to review what the school was doing and provide a blueprint for the future and I thought it would be a vote of confidence in what the school was doing.
> (Headteacher, Midchester Secondary)

Some senior staff considered the inspection especially timely for appraising recently introduced changes.

> I thought it would be a good thing. I recognized that the school had brought in a lot of innovations and that we had moved too quickly. It would be good therefore to have outsiders to look at what we were doing and provide a yardstick.
> (Deputy headteacher, Alderman King Secondary)

Whatever anxiety the managers of the schools felt was largely about the timing of the inspection; in a small number of cases this was considered inappropriate in coming 'just after Open Week', for example, or 'just after Christmas'.

By contrast with senior staff, classroom teachers were much more likely to admit to having been anxious about the forthcoming inspection. A minority of teachers did, however, claim that they had not been unduly concerned. Differences between teachers were frequently apparent. For example, some teachers in St Peter's Junior School thought that the inspection would be 'quite a positive process', 'an opportunity to get some things sorted out'; others were more negative. The news had aroused 'panic about the preparation needed' and suspicion that the aim was 'to pick up faults'. Such fears were common throughout the schools we studied. Indeed even supported self-evaluations (as carried out in Sedley) were not immune from them.

In some cases anxieties were associated with unfavourable experiences of inspectors and inspections in the past. Conversely where previous experiences had been more favourable, staff were generally more relaxed. Anxiety tended to be more apparent among those who were recently qualified, newly appointed, in 'acting' roles, unclear about what inspection entailed, or less confident about implementing the National Curriculum.

Inspectors adopted various strategies to deal with anxieties. Pre-inspection meetings, for example, between members of the inspection team and school staff were generally considered to have been useful in clearing up problems and reducing staff anxieties. Some headteachers and deputies were also thought to have played a significant part. The headteacher of Midchester Secondary had attended a local course on OFSTED inspections and had fed back the insights gained at a meeting with heads of department. This had been important in allaying some of the anxieties about the coming inspection.

One major task for the schools, in the period prior to inspectors arriving in the school, was the production and collation of a range of school information. Much of this information was not easily and readily available. The information-gathering activity and the involvement in meetings with inspectors to plan the inspection arrangements took a considerable amount of time. The brunt of this was borne by the headteacher and deputy. In the majority of non-OFSTED inspections estimates of the total amount of additional work required of senior staff ranged from one to four day-equivalents. Inspections carried out in accordance with the OFSTED Framework tended to demand more preparation time (one to twelve day-equivalents).

A measure of preparation was also required on the inspectors' side. Inspection team leaders were particularly heavily involved in preparing for the inspection. Even in the non-OFSTED cases estimated times ranged from one to four day-equivalents. Preparation for inspections carried out using the Framework required from four to ten day-equivalents with secondary inspections demanding more time than the primary. The amount of time other inspectors were involved was generally the equivalent of one or two days; in a few cases, however, estimates were as high as four or five days.

Thoughts before an inspection tended to be influenced by the extent to which a school was known to an inspector. Although some team members had little or no prior knowledge most knew at least some staff professionally. In some cases the school inspector[6] was a member of the team and generally had clear expectations of what could emerge. Occasionally local 'politics' was seen as a potentially sensitive factor:

All inspections have their foibles. There was a list of small 'p' politics associated with St Mark's . . . I was concerned to do a cast-iron job in evidence-gathering and did not wish to get embroiled in the politics which was essentially about the school becoming a 'breeding ground' for the high school which has the same chair of governors as St Mark's.

(Inspection team leader)

In general few anxieties were expressed apart from some inspectors being conscious of assuming the role of team leader or deputy team leader or operating under the new Framework for the first time.

Questions of how well inspectors knew each other, whether they had worked together on inspections before and the extent to which they valued each other's professional skills seemed important in anticipating how an inspection team would 'gel' in practice. An early feeling of *esprit de corps* was very apparent amongst the Forestshire team in its initial planning meeting for the Carlow school inspection. There is nothing particularly remarkable about the anxieties expressed by inspectors and teachers in the run-up to the inspection 'event'. Indeed, to those versed in the rigours of dramatic productions such preparations and rehearsals would merely seem necessary precursors of subsequent 'performances'. It is of interest, therefore, that they were almost invariably experienced as considerable disruptions to normal routines.

Reactions during inspection

All of the schools we studied also experienced some anxiety during their inspection. The headteacher of Alderman King Secondary discerned a variation in staff's reactions throughout the inspection week. 'The first couple of days there was an artificial euphoria – a "Dunkirk spirit". By midweek, niggles rose to the surface; for example, teachers were saying, "I wasn't seen enough" – a sort of midweek blues. At the end of the week people were saying they quite enjoyed their inspection.'

In Murbank Primary, as we have already seen, the collective dynamic was quite different. There, as the inspection progressed, anxieties mounted as the concerns of the inspectors became increasingly apparent. By the end of the week the headteacher and staff were in a state of severe shock.

In the large majority of our schools the pattern of general reaction was much less obvious and the level of anxiety often differed considerably from one teacher to another, even in the same school. Some teachers claimed to be unaffected by the presence of inspectors while others admitted to experiencing varying degrees of panic and, in one case, sleepless nights during the inspection period.

Much of the teachers' anxiety appeared to be associated with being observed teaching. One teacher at St Peter's Junior said: 'We were worried because we never knew how many inspectors would be in classes and for how long. Also worried about what they were actually looking for. We were constantly on edge.' Interestingly, some worries seemed to be a feature of all the variants we studied. Similar anxiety could arise in supported self-evaluations where the 'inspectors' included school staff. One teacher at Fenby Junior, for example, had been very conscious of the headteacher 'sitting in the corner like a tutor on teaching practice'. These kinds of anxiety are less likely to be felt by headteachers and senior staff since teaching is not the central aspect of their role. 'I felt calm because as a headteacher I wasn't going to be looked at as a teacher,' the head of Milton Primary told us. 'I lost no sleep over it.'

Inspection is based on the assumption that it is sampling what the school is *really* like. How far did teachers see things in the same way? Some admitted to putting on a 'special show' for the benefit of inspectors; others claimed that they treated the lesson being observed as a 'normal' one. Inspectors' views on this issue, meanwhile, were regarded as inconsistent by some teachers. '[Inspectors] said they didn't want to see showpiece lessons but during the inspection one said, "To score a [grade] one you have to put on a mega-galactic happening" ' (teacher, Potterton Secondary). One head of department at Midchester Secondary was moved to say that in future teachers in the department would be advised 'to do their best lessons during an inspection'.

With different teachers responding in different ways to the challenge of being inspected it is clear that inspectors need to develop sophisticated strategies for getting at 'the reality'. Teachers were especially concerned if they were observed in a lesson which was considered atypical in any way; for example, being observed when 'covering' a lesson for another colleague or at the end of the afternoon with potentially lively classes.

Another area which often provoked anxiety was the lack of feedback at the end of a lesson on how it had been perceived by the inspector. Although the extent of feedback given varied from inspector to inspector, the major problem was the lack of time available to the inspector before moving on to the next lesson. This problem was particularly acute where only parts of lessons were observed.

Teachers also had clear views about the timetabling of classroom visits. They generally preferred to know when they would be observed and were disappointed (although also relieved) if, for any reason, inspectors could not be present as expected. Inspectors, by contrast, generally preferred the additional flexibility of not being constrained by a predetermined timetable.

Ensuring adequate coverage of the teaching going on in a school without over- or under-observing particular teachers was sometimes difficult.

> Some teachers were visited two or three times – for example, in order to see work across the years in departments with only two teachers. Also on 'pupil pursuit'[7] it is pot luck which teachers you observe – one newly appointed teacher had four visits. In contrast, in the science department of 13 staff the inspector was fully stretched to see everyone.
>
> (Inspection team leader, Laurels Secondary)

The change to the inspector's 'hat' evoked comments. Some teachers, with little previous experience of inspections, were dismayed at encountering inspectors, previously seen as 'friendly advisers', in what was now a more distant, inspectorial role. The role-shift created conflicts for them. Indeed, some thought that inspectors now held views contrary to those they formerly espoused: 'Inspectors are now emphasizing large group and classroom teaching and saying different things to what they argued for previously,' one teacher at Danbrook Primary told us. Overall, though, teachers' reactions to inspectors were generally favourable. Valued personal qualities included being unobtrusive, helpful, supportive, empathetic, sensitive, positive, flexible and willing to listen to teachers' concerns. In only two inspections was there any indication of an inspector being considered insensitive in dealing with a teacher.

There is an unwritten code of 'etiquette' to which teachers expect inspectors to conform, particularly when observing lessons. Inspectors who were somewhat aloof, did not involve themselves with the class (especially in primary schools), failed to introduce themselves and left classes without a 'goodbye' were less well regarded. However, where negative assessments were made of inspectors, these were usually associated with professional skills rather than personal attributes (although a sharp line cannot easily be drawn between the two).

Professional credibility, in particular, could be a key issue: 'The team didn't have specialists in one or two areas so reports in those areas lacked credibility,' said the headteacher at Laurels Secondary. 'For example, the music inspector inspected some of the English.' This headteacher also contrasted local inspectors somewhat unfavourably with HMI: 'If the inspectors had the "terrier-like" approach of HMI and their sophisticated methods and sharp minds then our report would have been less good . . . the inspectors didn't find out some things we knew were wrong.' The issue of 'credibility' was also occasionally mentioned by inspectors themselves. In the inspection of Ecclesley Secondary, for example, the team leader commented that some information gained had been inaccurate and that the 'credentials' of a (primary) inspector had been challenged by the school.

Inspectors could also experience anxiety during an inspection. Those involved in using the OFSTED Framework for the first time were conscious of 'wanting to do it right'. One inspector at Midchester Secondary articulated what may be a general underlying fear: 'I always feel that we won't get the evidence and have time to sort it out. At the start I was optimistic and then became despondent, feeling that we won't get the task done. Then I became a lot more optimistic.' Another likened the uncertainties of inspection to an emerging detective story: 'An inspection gets the adrenalin going but is demanding in getting a vast quantity of information together and making it accessible. Inspection is like a detective story where you have to find strands and find the heart of a school' (team leader, Trenton Storrs Middle inspection). A common comment of headteachers and their staff was that inspection was a physically exhausting experience. Inspectors also found the process – involving not only full days but also late nights spent reflecting on and analysing the evidence collected – fatiguing and pressured. This was particularly felt by those involved in OFSTED-style inspections which were considered to be 'much more frenetic' than LEAs' former approaches.

We have spent some time considering the detailed reactions of inspected and inspectors to the inspection process. To some, such attention will seem unnecessary. Inspectors, they might argue, can 'see through' the various layers to the 'heart of the school'. Of course there is some anxiety but this rarely presents problems. There is an underlying reality which it is the inspectors' task to 'dig out'. The procedures are sufficiently tried-and-tested to survive the inevitable differences of experience and interpretation which emerge *en route*.

An alternative view might see things in a more subtle and provisional kind of way. The school's 'performance' during the 'inspection week' is a more chancy affair. It is subject to the subtleties (and vagaries) of the key participants, the extent to which the teachers 'rehearse' and the coherence of the teachers' and senior management's 'direction'. What emerges, pursuing the metaphor of the drama, is a 'performance'. That performance is the product of numerous interactions between teachers, pupils and inspectors, each of which is subject to interpretation. Circumstances may well arise in which the (mis)interpretation of nuance upon nuance results in an inappropriate picture being given of the whole institution.

Our own position falls somewhere between the two alternatives. Inspection procedures can be relatively 'robust' although doubtless they could be made more so. On the other hand the apparent precision with which inspection judgements are sometimes delivered can be misleading. Little of the language of inspection reports is couched in provisional or probabilistic terms. The possibility that a second chance to 'perform' could have led to a different set of interpretations is rarely (if ever) admitted.

Why does all this matter? One answer would be that the perceived 'status' of the inspection's findings will crucially affect their subsequent fate. A school which feels it has been given a 'fair chance' is more likely to take on the implications than one which *feels* differently.

Reactions to inspection findings

There were major differences in the ways schools reacted to inspection findings and recommendations. The inspection of Trenton Storrs Middle, for example, had a profound effect on the headteacher, who said: 'The inspection was very useful, it made me rethink fundamentally the organization of the curriculum.' This, however, was an exceptional comment. The common response in schools was that inspection – although it had highlighted, reinforced or confirmed issues that had already been identified – had not resulted in any 'real surprises'. Some headteachers even suggested that being surprised would have indicated a fault on their part. This perhaps reflected a belief in the omniscience of the 'good' headteacher. This lack of surprises led one head of department in Prince Edward Secondary to raise the question whether the inspectors 'have reflected the image we ourselves have put forward and, in the time available, can they do anything more than this?'

In some of the pre-OFSTED inspections the headteacher had been able to suggest some of the aspects for inspection. These were very often ones about which the headteacher had some prior concern and so in those cases 'no surprises' was a likely outcome. However, even in the more tightly prescribed OFSTED inspections a similar response was generally heard from headteachers and their staff:

> A good senior management team should know all the strengths and weaknesses of their school. Therefore there shouldn't be any surprises, nor should there be anything new, different or anything which can be construed as being major contributions to finding out about the school in

an inspection. What a full-scale OFSTED-type inspection does is to give a fairly comprehensive set of data on the quality of teaching and learning across the school and in each subject, which would be very difficult to achieve by any other means.

(Headteacher, Ladywell Secondary)

Nevertheless, on further probing, headteachers and others often did admit to some personal surprises and a realization that some areas had come off worse or better than had been expected. The headteacher of Ecclesley Secondary, for example, admitted to learning two things about the school: that the libraries were closed during the lunch break and that some pupils were unsympathetic towards others with special educational needs.

There were also cases where, despite a general acceptance of an inspection report, teachers continued to contest some individual findings or recommendations. In Ecclesley Secondary the headteacher rejected the inspectors' view that the withdrawal scheme for corrective reading was denying children their National Curriculum entitlement. The headteachers of Alderman King and Potterton schools remained unconvinced of the importance ascribed in both inspection reports to detailed job descriptions as a pre-requisite for effective line management.

In general, although specific aspects were queried, in a majority of the inspections most headteachers and their staffs broadly accepted the findings. Rejection of the findings as a whole, as was initially the case in Murbank Primary, was exceptional. A common belief was that the inspections had given a 'seal of approval' to recent initiatives and a general 'morale boost' for teachers. Some headteachers and their staff tended to feel that reports strengthened their positions and lent weight to existing and proposed developments. 'The inspection has given us some hard evidence on departments for use in the curriculum review. It has provided some bullets to fire and I am grateful for that,' said the headteacher at Alderman King Secondary. Some staff felt that the long term value of their inspection was limited because of the lack of subsequent support and advice. However, while this was something which LEAs would have liked to have provided it was often precluded by pressures on advisory resources.[8]

The extent to which inspectors were surprised by the findings was related to their prior knowledge of the school. Those who had such prior knowledge were in some cases surprised about certain aspects, sometimes pleasantly so. For example, the team leader of the Laurels Secondary inspection found that preconceptions about the headteacher's style had not been borne out by staff comments and that the school was performing better than had been expected. The vast majority of inspectors were in little doubt about the value of inspection for providing an agenda for the further development of the schools involved. Inspections were also seen as providing potentially useful information for the planning functions of their LEAs.

Inspection, anxiety and the 'self'

There is little doubt that most teachers find an inspection is an occasion of anxiety and stress. Such feelings are possibly endemic to the very concept of inspection embodying as it does associations with the hated 'payment by results' system of an earlier era. However, contributory factors other than the purely historical are likely to be more potent. Much of the anxiety touches something fundamental and enduring in the teacher psyche – the reluctance to be observed teaching, even amounting to fear in some cases. This in turn is perhaps related to the special characteristics of the act of teaching:

> Teaching combines privacy, autonomy and immediacy to an unusual degree. No act infringes these three properties so completely as inspection by an unknown observer. Full formal inspection applies that infringement on the scale of the whole institution and does so within a limited span of time.
>
> (Pearce 1986b: 134–5)

To be observed teaching is to present a window on to the self. The act of teaching lies at the heart of the teacher's sense of professional and personal identity and self-esteem. When teaching competence is perceived to be wanting a major aspect of the teacher's life-purpose can be brought into question. As one teacher at Murbank Primary said, 'If this report is true I should never have been in the job.'

Even the prospect of being found wanting in this respect is likely to cause anxiety, perhaps the more so with those who feel themselves to be good teachers. Most teachers want to be seen at their best and tend to be unhappy if they are observed taking atypical classes, if they think that inspectors do not 'see things as they do', and particularly if they cannot establish rapport with the inspector by explaining the context of their teaching and receiving feedback about it.

Headteachers and other senior staff seem generally less prone to expressions of anxiety on their *own* account. This may, in part, be due to the fact that they are less directly involved in classroom teaching. Their professional identity is more likely to be seen in terms of management and school leadership. These qualities are much less visible than those associated with teaching. It is not so easy to observe management 'happening' in quite the direct way that is possible for teaching. Inspectors are much more reliant on inferring the nature of management from its traces in other evidence.

In addition, management is a responsibility that is shared with at least some other senior staff. In other words, the core role of specific senior staff remains largely free of direct exposure in 'real time'. This is not to say that headteachers and others do not experience anxiety, especially where they have good reason for anticipating a very critical report. When such a report actually appears, post-inspection anxiety may be high for all staff and the headteacher particularly, as shown in the inspection of Murbank Primary.

Further support for the finding that anxiety is more often associated with classroom teachers than with headteachers and senior staff is provided by a questionnaire survey of 35 secondary OFSTED inspections (Brimblecombe *et al.* 1995a). Follow-up interviews in this survey also suggested a further reason for the discrepancy – that classroom teachers felt left out of the planning process and therefore felt less familiar with inspection and less in control. It is undoubtedly the case that knowledge of the inspection process and involvement in its planning reflects the internal hierarchy of the school. It is the headteacher, deputy and other senior staff who participate with the inspectors in planning the details and organization of an inspection. They, in turn, involve the next tier of management in planning the inspection of subject areas and other aspects of the school. Finally the classroom teachers may be heavily reliant for information and guidance from those above them in the hierarchy.

Of course, much can be done to equalize this asymmetry of knowledge. Inspectors will meet the whole staff before an inspection to explain its purpose and what is involved. Headteachers and senior staff can also build on this process through talks and other forms of ongoing support.

A headteacher speaks

Nonetheless, we continued to find evidence of the persistence of teacher anxiety even in schools which received very good inspection reports. This is illustrated in the extended interview sequence below obtained from the headteacher of Low Moors Secondary, which was inspected in the second year of the OFSTED programme (1994/5).

> *Headteacher (HT)*: It's hugely stressful, because you know so far in advance of the inspection [so] you're trying to prepare more and more and more . . . You had such a long while to prepare beforehand, I mean I actually knew Christmas Eve of last year! Almost a year to the actual week of the inspection. And I think because obviously schools are anxious to try to do their best you just keep adding to it all the time . . . there were two car loads of documentation that went from here.
>
> *Interviewer (I)*: You mean literally two car loads?
>
> *HT*: Yes, literally two car loads. I mean huge crates . . . because you needed to do everything back over the last five years, including all the finance, all the curriculum, all the schemes of work.
>
> *I*: So you didn't put anything extra in?
>
> *HT*: No, it was just what they were asking for. The headteacher's form had been cut down considerably since the first pilot OFSTEDs but even so we actually produced reams and reams of paperwork. Then from there on in you're actually working with your teams to start to make sure that the policy's actually in practice . . . It kind of builds up because you think, 'Oh yes, I had better do that and I'd better do this,' and as much as you try and stay calm by the time you get to the actual week people are very much on edge . . .
>
> *HT*: [on the inspection week itself] It's rather like taking your driving test every lesson because the person who's in the room is there with the clipboard, with the, you know, non-expression face. You don't know whether they're ticking because it's all right or ticking because there's something wrong. They go out in the middle of a double lesson so you and the children are left bemused as to whether it was alright, awful or very very good. You just don't know where you are. Some colleagues

got to the state of ... nervous exhaustion because of not knowing when somebody's coming into the room. Every time an inspector goes by the door you were thinking, 'Ooh, it's me.' And some people were seen seven times during the week and some people were not seen at all ...

I think somebody could have actually just have said 'look, on Monday we'll be going into these lessons, on Tuesday we'll be going into these ...' But it was lack of feedback that was the awful thing about it all. We didn't know where we were going, we didn't know what we were doing.

I: You mean feedback at the end of the lesson?

HT: Yes, nothing. I mean you don't get anything.

Low Moors, by all accounts, was performing very well indeed.

It may be that the wide availability of the OFSTED Handbook will eventually help to demystify the process of inspection. Moreover, if the OFSTED system continues into the future then the process will become more familiar and this may in turn reduce levels of anxiety still further. Likewise the continuance of teacher appraisal, which also includes an element of classroom observation, may help to make at least this aspect of inspection less of a concern. It is doubtful, however, whether feelings of anxiety could be totally eliminated. A reasonable level of anxiety may generate appropriate 'arousal' to help teachers perform well. The real issue is to ensure that inspection does not lead to widespread debilitation and even despair.

Inspection: an example of work 'intensification'?

Another factor contributing to anxiety and stress is the additional work that being inspected generates for teachers. This arises not only during the inspection week itself but also in the period beforehand. Indeed, Brimblecombe and her colleagues (1995a) suggest that the latter is the more stressful period, starting from the notification of an OFSTED inspection and building up over a term or more as the inspection draws nearer.

As we have seen much of the preparation for an inspection falls on the headteacher and senior management. This task is much heavier for OFSTED than for previous forms of inspection. Detailed lists of documents have to be assembled (and often created) for despatch to the RgI in advance of the inspection. Additional preparation also extends to the staff who will be involved in ensuring that policies, schemes of work and the like are all in place. The availability of the Handbook provides a detailed model to which schools may feel they have to conform. Excessive and obsessive preparation can be the result extending, at least for some teachers, into the inspection week itself.

Reactions to inspection may be regarded as another manifestation of the 'intensification' hypothesis which has been proposed in recent years (Hargreaves 1994: 117–38). This sees teachers' work having become 'increasingly intensified, with teachers expected to respond to greater pressures and comply with multiple innovations under conditions that are at best stable and at worst deteriorating'. Inspection is one in a long line of externally-imposed account-ability demands and interventions experienced by teachers throughout the 1980s and 1990s which have, arguably, lengthened their working week.

Hargreaves suggests that '[t]he demands of accountability and intensifi-cation can be felt particularly harshly where they embody singular views of correct (and by implication, incorrect) practice' (1994: 149). Such singular, as opposed to multiple views, of competence 'may mesh poorly with the teacher's personal self or with the context in which the teacher works' (1994: 150) and are likely to generate anxiety. This is, of course, the case with inspection which is an instrument of accountability based on a detailed specification (especially in OFSTED inspections) of what constitutes the 'good' school.

Intensification and inspectors

The intensification thesis has been argued in relation to teachers but it also throws some interesting light on recent developments in the work of inspec-tors. In the past, inspectors (particularly those in LEAs) had considerable pro-fessional autonomy in developing the nature of their role. The amount of time devoted to the core tasks (of curriculum support and development, INSET, general advice and support to schools, and inspection and evaluation) varied considerably both between and within teams, as did the approaches adopted.

Throughout the 1980s this freedom of operation was progressively reduced as inspectors increasingly became local agents promoting the multiple cur-riculum and INSET initiatives of central government. More and more time was spent making bids for government grants and subsequently managing the delivery and evaluation of these new initiatives. Inspectors were also frequently involved in the programmes of school closures and staff redeployment associ-ated with the decline in pupil numbers throughout the decade. Meeting these new responsibilities, whilst at the same time trying to maintain the traditional role of general adviser to schools, resulted in high levels of work and stress for many inspectors.

The intensification process continued further into the 1990s as increasing proportions of LEA funds were transferred to schools through schemes of local management and, following the 1992 Act, to OFSTED for financing the new system of inspection. This meant that LEA inspectors effectively had to finance themselves through 'buy back' of their services by schools and successfully winning OFSTED inspection contracts.

As far as the purely inspection aspect of their role is concerned inspectors are now required to follow the very detailed prescriptions of the Handbook. The freedom to determine what to inspect and how to inspect has effectively been withdrawn in favour of an imposed single approach which seeks to codify, rou-tinize and standardize the inspection process. Extending the comprehensive-ness of inspection (both in terms of schools and content coverage), while at the same time compressing the timescales for completing inspections, has resulted in inspectors working under greater pressures than hitherto. Almost without exception inspectors report that inspections are time-consuming, stressful and involve working long hours. Repeatedly working at such a pace also calls into question the soundness of the judgements made under such conditions.[9]

Another problem is that some RgIs feel that inspection compresses so much into a relatively short time that they are left with insufficient opportunity to reflect properly on the data:

> At the end of the week I'm not sure I haven't just skimmed it and I'm not sure whether that's a reflection on me as an individual. But I would need to be able to construct, de-construct and then re-construct the information that I've got to test it all out. And you really can't do that . . . By about the Thursday or Friday what you really want to do is go away for a week and then three or four of you come back.
>
> (RgI, Low Moors Secondary)

Inspection: novel insights?

Inspection represents a major intervention in the life of a school which places considerable demands on those involved. The costs of inspection are considerable – as much as £20,000 or more in the case of large secondary schools. The real costs of inspection, taking account of the additional work required of teachers and also of inspectors (outside of that for which they are formally contracted) will be even higher. Despite this considerable investment of human and other resources the outcomes, in terms of enhanced knowledge or insightful understanding of the nature of individual schools, appear to be limited, at least for the greater majority of school staff.

It seems that only in a minority of cases is teachers' knowledge of schools fundamentally changed and this is often where inspection reveals substantial weaknesses. Although no doubt some schools in this latter category are aware of their parlous condition others are not. For example, the inspectors' disclosures to the staff of Murbank Primary did appear to come as an unwelcome surprise and resulted, at least initially, in their rejection. The Murbank inspection is particularly interesting since it also revealed the difficulty senior staff had in accepting that poor standards of teaching and curriculum organization were possible in a school characterized by good personal relationships between teachers and pupils. A similar view was also apparent in a couple of other primary school inspections where the situation was less serious. It may be, as Hargreaves (1994: 146) suggests, that for many primary teachers the commitment to goals of care and nurturance take precedence over others which are more specifically educational.

Perhaps the gaining of significant insights is unlikely given the scope of inspection and the limited time in which it has to be carried out. 'There could be a problem in trying to cover all aspects in a report and unearthing complex areas of life which one ought to understand – so the temptation would not be to dig too deep. The Framework has to be "fed", so you daren't be too focused' (CI, Hilltown LEA). Another possible explanation is that the assumed 'common-sense' and 'taken for granted' model of the school which underpins inspection tends to suppress the emergence of original insights. Perhaps, as the

RgI for the Low Moor Secondary inspection argues below, the use of interpretative frameworks would be more productive:

RgI: I think the more helpful insights you can have into the way in which a school works does depend on you interpreting what's going on rather than just trying to record it.

I: Of course it's rather ironic isn't it, that the whole thing is called a Framework.

RgI: Yes, absolutely, and it's not. It's . . . certainly not a theoretical framework, in fact it is designed not to be. It's designed to stop people using different theoretical frameworks . . . [But] I think it's that which enables you to have the more interesting and I hope more purposeful dialogue with managers in schools . . .

I: Supposing you hadn't had that sort of prohibition, what sort of framework would you have found helpful?

RgI: I tend to use 'systems theory' sort of frameworks . . . Schools are essentially so 'loosely coupled' that the only feedback tends to be exam results or performance indicators and an OFSTED inspection, and what they ought to be looking at is building different sorts of feedback mechanisms within school so you really know what's happening.

Despite these reservations, the vast majority of inspections were generally regarded as having been valuable. The frequent references to confirming what was already known, identifying priorities and raising morale and confidence should not be underestimated. Here is a headteacher talking of the experience of being inspected in the first year of the OFSTED primary school programme:

Unexpectedly what I learned of substance was that we were a better school than I thought we were . . . I hadn't realized to what extent because recent developments in education have taken me more out of the classroom and immediate first hand contact with staff and pupils. I think ten years ago you might have been more aware that the staff were planning meticulously, I know they plan meticulously but I didn't know to what extent this was high quality planning as distinct from the whole spectrum which OFSTED sees.

I think the overall learning experience for me was that it raised our self-esteem and our confidence as a school enormously and particularly for myself, because in this job you tend to be criticized from all quarters and you tend to be self-critical as well if you are conscientious. It was a nice opportunity really to be able to think 'yes, someone has praised us over quite a wide field'.

(Headteacher, Broad Lane Primary)

This headteacher went on to explain that the teachers had prepared their lessons more fully than usual during the inspection and felt, as a consequence, that they had especially enjoyed their teaching.

In contrast to teachers, inspectors clearly learned much of substance about individual schools particularly, of course, where they had little or no prior knowledge of them. Even where they did know something of a school beforehand they found that inspection increased that knowledge very considerably. Not infrequently inspectors also commented that their existing views of schools were not necessarily borne out on inspection.

The value of inspection, however, is not only to be assessed by the extent to which it provides new knowledge and insights about schools. At least equally important is whether inspection leads to change and, more significantly, real improvement of schools. It is to this issue that we turn in later chapters. But first we examine in more detail the methods which inspectors employ and the claims for the validity of inspection.

6 THE METHODOLOGICAL PROBLEMS OF INSPECTION

There are more things in heaven and earth, Horatio,
Than are dreamt of in your philosophy
(Shakespeare, *Hamlet*)

Professor Stewart Sutherland, the first of Her Majesty's Chief Inspectors (HMCI) under OFSTED, was very clear about the role of the inspectors. When commending for consultation the *Draft Framework for the Inspection of Schools* (DFE 1992b) in the summer of 1992 he stated: 'Inspectors are there to formulate and present a picture of the school as it really is; to judge how well a school is meeting the various demands placed upon it and the needs of its pupils. They are not there as amateur philosophers, psychologists or sociologists of education' (Sutherland 1992).

His comment expresses a major assumption underlying the inspection process – namely that inspection provides a 'true' picture of a school. This 'picture' theory of school inspection rests on two further assumptions: first a belief in an essential entity, 'the school as it really is'; and second, a belief that this entity is knowable and can be represented in written form as an inspection report.

The implication of the second sentence in the quotation above is that 'the school as it really is' can be directly apprehended without the need for any *theoretical* interpretation. In other words, the use of specialized psychological, philosophical, or sociological concepts is not necessary for revealing the essential nature of schools. Presumably all is apparent to the discerning eye of the inspector. We know, however, that no observer and no observation can be untainted by theory. Observation is not a neutral act – selection and interpretation are inevitably involved and these reflect prior theoretical perspectives, even if these are not formally recognized and made explicit.

Model of the school

Inspection necessarily entails a conception of what are regarded as the essential features of schools 'as they really are'. Such features are assumed to be relatively stable over time. Clearly, if they were not, and changed significantly from one moment to the next, then description would be difficult if not impossible. This notion of stability is assumed to carry over into the future, at least for that period between the end of the inspection and the appearance of the report. An inspection, however, always marks a potential point of discontinuity at which the school may move, in acting on the report's recommendations, from one state to another.

There has been a trend in recent years for the essential features to be embodied implicitly, if not explicitly, in inspection handbooks. The most developed form to date is that of the OFSTED Handbook. The features it describes are considered to be the discrete, invariant and defining characteristics of schools. They are also generally reflected in the basic format of inspection reports. In the past the features chosen to describe schools varied somewhat from inspectorate to inspectorate. The OFSTED Framework has now effectively imposed a universal set of features. These, as outlined earlier, constitute a specific model of the school which might be described as a 'multi-level, performance, process, context' model.

It is 'multi-level' because descriptions are provided in the inspection report at different levels of generality. The first consists of the separate accounts of each curriculum and cross-curriculum area. The detail of the first level is effectively summarized in the more general accounts of the second level as: standards and quality; efficiency; pupils' development and behaviour. The third and highest level of generality is the summary represented by the main findings and key issues for action.

Standards, quality, efficiency, development and behaviour are also expressions of the concept of 'performance'. 'Process' aspects are recognized in a number of school-wide features (quality of teaching, quality and range of the curriculum, etc.) which are considered to be influences on the school's performance. Finally the 'context' is communicated through the provision of a range of school data and statistical indicators.

Whatever the protestations, this model is not, of course, 'theory-free'. Notions of 'quality', 'standards' and 'efficiency' draw on aspects of management theory. Further ideas are also derived from 'theories' of the curriculum and the organization of schools associated with government educational policy and HMI practice respectively. The OFSTED model is but one among many that could be envisaged. Indeed, even within the parameters of the 1992 Act it would have been possible to devise other models – other ways, that is, of deciding what the fundamental lineaments of schools should be and how they should be understood.

Different models produce different descriptions of a school. OFSTED inspections, however, do not acknowledge this potential diversity and present, in effect, a belief in one best approach. What support is there for the model? In the Framework and Handbook the model of the school and the approach to inspection are not separated analytically. As a result, the issue has not been posed in the way that we do here and so the question cannot be answered directly.

Some indirect evidence is to hand. The review of the first hunded OFSTED inspections of secondary schools found that the Framework and Handbook had been well received in the schools inspected (OFSTED 1994c). Headteachers considered them to be a useful management tool and teachers generally welcomed the publication of the criteria for judging teaching and learning. So it might be argued that tacit support had been given to the OFSTED model. The only indication of any overt questioning was that some headteachers, including those of several middle schools inspected, 'were less satisfied with what they perceived to be the narrow constraints of a sharply defined curricular Framework' (OFSTED 1994c: 12).

The same study also found that RgIs were favourably inclined towards both documents. There was no indication of dissatisfaction with the underlying conception of the school. Where there were concerns these were generally about logistical and other aspects for the arrangements for inspection. As mentioned earlier we found similar responses in our interviews with LEA chief inspectors. The generally favourable reception of the documents has also been noted in a survey of the first 100 primary, special and nursery schools inspected (OFSTED 1995b). Although OFSTED has been diligent in responding to criticisms, and revising the documents as a consequence, it is significant that the basic model has remained intact – initially extended and elaborated in detail admittedly but not fundamentally changed.[1]

So how has this situation of tacit acceptance come about? The model of the school which OFSTED presents is recognizably set within a 'management systems' perspective. This is a perspective, of course, which has received increasing emphasis in educational policy in the last twenty or so years. As a consequence the discourses of management have progressively displaced other lexicons for describing and understanding schools (Ball 1994). It is, therefore, perhaps not surprising that the OFSTED conception, which is wholly consistent with those discourses, has been considered unexceptional.

The Handbook presents with great magisterial confidence an analysis of the school in terms of apparently self-evident structures and outcomes. There is little indication that notions of standards, quality and efficiency and the other terms of the lexicon are endemically contestable. It is, however, the OFSTED text which inspectors now have to follow. In doing so they are involved in collecting evidence and analysing and interpreting it in accordance with the model in the Handbook. Thus when an inspection report is produced it might be said to be a description of a school 'as it really is *from the perspective of the OFSTED model*'. This is, of course, equivalent to expressing confidence in a report's 'validity'.

The question of validity ultimately turns on the kind of evidence which inspectors collect and how that evidence is transformed into the descriptions and judgements which constitute the report. Such a question is therefore about the methods, procedures and assumptions of inspection practice – in a word, about the methodology adopted.

The methodology of inspection

There has been very little critical study of the methodology of inspection and even less based upon any empirical research. One aspect, however, which has attracted some research interest is that of inspectors' judgements. Gray and Hannon (1986) looked at the judgements made on examination results by HMI in its reports of individual schools. Elliott and Ebbutt (1986), also using HMI reports, attempted to make explicit the criteria on which inspectors' judgements were based. More recently, Nixon and Rudduck (1993), in an interview study of LEA inspectors, have argued the need for a clearer understanding of professional judgement and the authority by which it is exercised.

We turn now to look at methodological concerns in rather more detail, drawing again on data from our case studies and interviews with chief inspectors. Not surprisingly, different inspectors had different concerns. It is necessary first, however, to reiterate a general point about the nature of inspection. Although inspections may differ externally in such matters as duration, comprehensiveness and involvement of school staff they are, nevertheless, very similar in terms of the activities involved (observing classes, looking at pupils' work, talking to teachers and feedback to senior staff; see Maychell and Keys 1993: 19).

It is important to realize therefore that although inspection is now virtually synonymous with the OFSTED approach, the methodology which it embodies is not *fundamentally* different from that which underlay the inspection practice of HMI and local inspectorates in the recent past. OFSTED's distinctive contribution has been to make the methodology of inspection explicit in unprecedented detail and publicly accessible through the Handbook (OFSTED 1992b; 1993b; 1994b; 1995a).

The dominance of observation

Most comments made about inspection tend to be concerned with classroom observation. This is not surprising given that it is the one method which all teachers directly encounter. It is also the method which occupies the majority of the inspectors' time – the Handbook recommends that a minimum of 60 per cent of time be spent this way (OFSTED 1994b: 12).

From the mid-1970s onwards HMI developed the use of structured forms for recording the essential features of lessons. Similar forms or *aides-memoire* were also used by some LEA inspectorates. These forms do not require that inspectors use the highly specific 'low inference' categories of observation which have been developed by some researchers.[2] Such observation schedules would probably be impractical given the large volume of classroom visits made over a short period of time which inspection is seen to require. Researchers' schedules also tend to focus on a narrow band of behaviours which are not necessarily those of greatest educational interest. Instead inspectors tend to record their observations under more holistic or 'high inference' categories such as 'quality of learning'.[3]

These ideas have been further developed in the Handbook with the use of the 'lesson observation form' (LOF). The LOF consists of an A4 sheet which allows inspectors to organize their comments under the headings of achievement, quality of learning and the quality of teaching. A particularly significant feature is that each of the judgements made under the headings is summarized as a rating on a five-point scale. An overall lesson grade is also given. The grading of judgements in this way is an elaboration of HMI's former practice.

The LOFs concerned with individual curriculum areas are summarized and ratings aggregated on 'subject evidence forms'. Observations made in arenas other than classrooms are recorded on 'supplementary evidence forms'.

Other sources of evidence

A variety of documentation is available to inspectors. Much of this is provided by the school and consists of descriptive information and statistical data. OFSTED also provides a 'pre-inspection context and school indicator' (PICSI) report which explains how to set the school in its local context and how to compare it with other schools. Documentation serves two broad purposes: to formulate a pre-inspection commentary and to identify issues for subsequent inspection; and also to help validate judgements emerging from other sources of evidence. Some inspectors we interviewed recognized that the more systematic use of documents as required by the Handbook was not a self-evident process and that their approach to the task needed 'beefing up'.

A special case of the use of school documentation is the scrutiny of a sample of pupils' work. Although inspectors had long followed this aspect of HMI practice, some felt that guidance was required for developing more rigorous procedures for assessing the level and appropriateness of the work. The concern for more guidance in this area was also expressed by many RgIs involved in the first OFSTED inspections (OFSTED 1994c).

Parents of a school to be inspected are invited to a specially convened meeting conducted by the RgI. The aim is to seek their views on a range of specific aspects (pupils' standards of work and behaviour, parental involvement, etc.). Parental views may also be sought by means of a standardized questionnaire developed by OFSTED.

Further evidence is obtained through discussion with teachers, governors and others involved in the work of the school. Although much was done through relatively informal talk, some inspectors felt the need to move towards more formal interviewing and to develop further their technique through the clearer formulation of questions or by otherwise improving existing interview instruments.

Inspection has always placed a high premium on the professional judgement of inspectors and the implicit notion of 'connoisseurship' (Kogan 1986). Increasingly, however, the trend has been to make the basis of connoisseurship explicit by identifying criteria and quantifying the resulting judgements by means of grading scales. This tendency has reached its most elaborated form to date in the OFSTED approach to inspection.

In addition to the grading of lessons, 'judgement recording statements' (JRSs) have to be completed (OFSTED 1994b: (3) 13–14; 59–60). A JRS consists of a stem followed by a seven-point scale defined by two semantic extremes (for example: excellent–very poor). Inspectors decide on which point of the scale their judgement lies.[4] JRSs are completed for the school as a whole and also for each curriculum area. Although a very large number of JRSs are defined not all are likely to be needed for every inspection. The purpose of JRSs is to help inspectors focus on the essential judgements they have to make although they are not substitutes for the judgements themselves. Responses to JRSs also assist OFSTED in retrieving judgements for use in the compilation of its reports on national trends and in monitoring the work of inspectors.

Inspection: threats to validity

In our interviews we asked teachers to comment on the adequacy of the methods which had been employed in the inspection of their schools. The same opportunity was extended to the inspectors. The general response from both groups was that the methods employed were considered broadly satisfactory and, in some cases, excellent. Even where schools received relatively less favourable reports criticisms were few and more usually related to the inspectors' style than to the detail of their methods. However, some concerns related directly or indirectly to inspection methods were voiced although no teacher, or inspector for that matter, developed much in the way of a sustained and detailed critique.

As a result of the similarity existing between inspections at a general methodological level, all are *potentially* at risk from several common threats to validity. We find that the vast majority of comments made about inspection methods can be related to questions of sampling, criteria, corroboration, or context. It must not be supposed, however, that all, or indeed any of these concerns necessarily manifest themselves in each and every inspection. What they represent are ways of summarizing the most frequent issues emerging from our interviews with the protagonists of inspection – teachers and inspectors.

Sampling

The Handbook states that the 'sample of lessons and classes inspected must constitute an adequate cross-section of the work of the school . . . be representative of all age and ability groups . . . Lessons should be seen in all [National Curriculum] subjects and in other subjects or aspects specified in the inspection contract' (OFSTED 1994b: (2) 11).

As already noted (page 54), ensuring adequate coverage without over- or under-observing particular teachers can be difficult in practice. In addition, unusual events during the inspection week can cause problems. For example, in the inspection of Alderman King Secondary a head of department remarked that the sample of Year 11 teachers and classes observed had been insufficient because 'mock' examinations were held on one of the days.

Even the adequate coverage of teachers and lessons will not necessarily ensure that all aspects of provision are encountered. There may be some things not going on during the inspection period which nevertheless do take place at other times. The inspectors of Midchester Secondary commented that they had not seen the rich multi-cultural provision which the context of the school had led them to expect. The headteacher explained that this was because the inspection week had not been a typical one. Equally there may be some things taking place which inspectors fail to see because, even with a large team, they cannot be everywhere all the time. Lessons and other school activities can only be sampled and the sample required could be as low as 7 per cent of all lessons in a large secondary school (OFSTED 1993b: (3) 11). Consequently inspectors need to be particularly cautious about saying that something (whether an aspect of the teaching, curriculum content or whatever) is *not* taking place solely on the basis of what *is* observed.

Decisions on what to observe may be changed as a result of unforeseen contingencies (for example, unexpected absence of a teacher) or in order to follow up a promising 'lead' in more detail. The pattern of sampling, therefore, needs to be monitored throughout to ensure that overall coverage will have been achieved by the end of the inspection.

Sampling was also an issue for other inspection methods. For example, in a few cases questions were raised about the adequacy of some of the samples of teachers chosen for interview. Inspectors at St Mark's Middle realized that they had interviewed insufficient subject coordinators to get a full picture of the curriculum arrangements in the school. At Carlow Secondary the sample of parents had been identified by the headteacher and the inspectors felt that it was both too small and biased towards the 'PTA stalwarts'.

The sampling of pupils' work was often regarded as one of the weaker aspects of inspection, both in terms of the difficulty of identifying a representative range and the limited time available for giving the work adequate consideration.

> Looking at pupils' work – you can do a fair bit as you go along. Getting a sample across the board is very valuable. In all honesty, though, the review of pupils' work is trivial and deserves a great deal more time. It would be better to spend a whole day on this using very clear criteria – the Framework and the time allocation trivializes this.
>
> (Chief Inspector, Oxley)

Criteria

Concern about criteria was expressed by some teachers involved in the non-OFSTED inspections. Teachers at Monkton Secondary, for example, felt some inspectors were unsure what they were looking for and that overall consistency was a crucial issue. This problem of inspectors working to different criteria was acknowledged by the team leader. In a couple of inspections teachers noted an inconsistency between current criteria and those employed during recent inspection visits by the local inspectorate (Tennyson Road Secondary) and HMI (Midchester Secondary).

One of the characteristics of the OFSTED approach is that criteria for major features of a school are specified in considerable detail. These take the form of short descriptive paragraphs or lists; for example, the criteria for judging the 'quality of teaching':

Teaching quality is to be judged by the extent to which:
- teachers have clear objectives for their lessons;
- pupils are aware of these objectives;
- teachers have a secure command of the subject;
- lessons have suitable content;
- activities are well chosen to promote learning of that content;
- teaching methods engage, motivate and challenge all pupils, enabling them to progress at a suitable pace, and to be aware of their achievements and progress.

(OFSTED 1994b: (2) 26)

Criteria are further amplified by the provision of contrasting paragraphs one of which describes a 'good' example of the feature, and the other where it is 'unsatisfactory'. In addition, guidance is provided on the issues to be considered when reviewing evidence and the factors to be taken account of when reaching a judgement. As a result of this amplification the number of effective criteria rapidly multiplies into double figures. This attempt to eliminate the scope for personal subjectivity, in this case by the formulation of explicit criteria, provides an example of what is known more generally as 'procedural objectivity'.

Teachers generally welcomed the use of OFSTED criteria. Inspectors also accepted the criteria as a useful development, although there was a feeling that they were in some cases rather 'woolly' and insufficiently precise.

An important issue apparent in the move towards greater explicitness arises from the fact that the criteria associated with a particular aspect are presumably not of equal importance. For example, the final criterion in the previous list (which is actually a composite of several criteria) is clearly of greater importance than the first. If this is so, how are the criteria to be combined into an overall judgement? This is particularly salient in a situation where some criteria are met but not all. The Handbook requires that overall judgements be graded on a five-point scale. The quality of teaching in individual lessons is to be graded as follows:

1 Many good features, some of them outstanding
2 Good features, and no major shortcomings
3 Sound
4 Some shortcomings in important areas
5 Many shortcomings.

(OFSTED 1994b: (3) 16)

How then are individual assessments on each criterion to be represented as a single numerical grade? Do the 'good features' mentioned in the first two points of the scale refer to the 'quality of teaching' criteria in the previous list? If so, how are differing assessments of the criteria converted into a single point on the scale? The Handbook does not say.

Some inspectors are confident in their ability to make such judgements and basically see no problem:

> I have a crib sheet, we all have a crib sheet so that against the lesson observation form we'd have the criteria we were looking for . . . and the levels that we'd be giving so that we'd do a quick check. But after you have done a lot, you know what you're looking at and what it is that you'd be giving them.
>
> (Inspector, Broad Lane Primary)

An RgI, however, had a rather different view:

> I think in the end inspectors make totally subjective judgements. They put the numbers in and then try to work out what text agrees with the numbers . . . They're writing down numbers and then going back to the Framework to make sure they're right in words that match the grade they've given . . . People are seeking to meet the needs of the Framework . . . it has to be internally consistent. That's all that matters.
>
> (RgI, Low Moors Secondary)

Another inspector observed that although OFSTED had published criteria these did not eliminate the possibility of different judgements being made *in practice*. In other words, the specification of criteria alone does not necessarily guarantee validity. Moreover, criteria can never be so tightly defined as to expel the act of judgement completely: 'Professional judgement may operate with reference to explicit criteria, but these cannot in themselves define – or circumscribe – a process which necessarily includes a strong tacit or inferential element' (Nixon and Rudduck 1993).

Context

As already noted, teachers frequently commented on the lack of time and opportunity they had to discuss with inspectors the lessons in which they were observed. This difficulty was also appreciated by the inspectors themselves. There were two issues here. The first was that teachers generally wished to know how their lessons had been perceived. The importance of providing feedback depends, as Hargreaves argues, on what is seen to be the main aim of inspection:

> Now if the primary purpose of inspection is to monitor the system or even to identify failing schools, low levels of feedback at the time of observation – the point where it is most likely to be useful – is tolerable. Where the primary purpose is improvement, this rejection of dialogue is indefensible.
>
> (Hargreaves 1995: 120)

The second issue was the need to explain the context of a lesson: one teacher at Danbrook Primary said they would 'like more time to explain to the inspector what was happening in the classroom'. Although this may be obviated in part by having a lesson plan available this could lead to further difficulties:

'Teaching had to be mapped out and rigidly kept to. Had to slow down the work on cress seeds so as to do it on time!' (Teacher, Playfair Primary).

The problem of ensuring dialogue between individual inspectors and teachers is particularly accentuated in OFSTED inspections where the amount to be seen is so great and where inspectors frequently have to resort to the tactic of observing parts of lessons only. The inspectors are therefore advised to '[e]xplain to headteachers and teachers that *periods of classroom observation are likely to vary in length* and must be adequate to gather sufficient evidence for the judgements made; but that they may not always be followed with some oral comment. A consistent approach must be adopted by members of an inspection team' (OFSTED 1995a: 12; our emphasis).

Some headteachers and senior staff stressed that the context of the school should be made explicit in the inspection report.

> The context/background was noted briefly but not taken into account. Most children are from council homes, many are extra-district – many moved to the school by parents who weren't satisfied. The school draws on one of the poorest areas in Falton.
>
> (Deputy headteacher, Murbank Primary)

Another aspect of context is the immediate history of a school. The history of a school helps to account for its current situation and description. If explicit recognition is not given in the report to significant developments which occurred before the inspection, then teachers are apt to regard the account of the school as unsatisfactory.

> It is not in the nature of inspection to have an historical basis. I am in my fourth year as head here and I can see enormous change having occurred, although much is not yet complete . . . You need to recognize the context and I think less of inspection because it doesn't.
>
> (Headteacher, Alderman King Secondary)

The Handbook gives some recognition of this concern for school context by requiring an introductory section in the inspection report which sets out details of the intake of pupils and the area served by the school and also provides specific school indicators. Further emphasis is given in the current revised (draft) version of the Framework which re-titles the introductory section as 'Characteristics of the School' and provides the following guidance:

> The report may refer briefly to any particularly significant features which help to set the inspection in context, for example, recent change of head or other staffing features, unusual accommodation, dramatic changes of roll, or a particular ability or ethnic profile of pupils. It may be appropriate to refer to the timing of the inspection if, for example, it coincides with the beginning of the school year or if the normal programme of the school is interrupted in some way.
>
> (OFSTED 1995c: 15–16)

The implicit assumption would seem to be that, with some knowledge of this kind of information, a reader will be able to set subsequent judgements encountered in the main body of the report into context. This is probably an unrealistic expectation.

The contextualization of individual judgements is attempted in the specific case of pupil achievement. In most lessons inspectors are expected to make a graded judgement on the appropriateness of pupils' achievements, taking into account their abilities (OFSTED 1994b: (3) 17). This requires two things of the inspector: knowledge of the relevant norms; and, equally importantly, knowledge of pupils' 'abilities'. To do this inspectors are to 'use as their reference for national expectations the NC Statutory Orders where they apply, and specialist knowledge and judgement' (OFSTED 1994b: (3) 17). As for their views of pupils' abilities these are to be formed 'on the basis of discussions with them and with staff, from evidence of previous assessments, consideration of grouping arrangements in relation to the school population and any other evidence which is available' (OFSTED 1994b: (3) 17).

The task facing inspectors in making such assessments on dozens of different lessons is formidable and raises doubts about the precision and consistency possible between inspectors. One RgI identified the problem of over- and under-grading:

> [I]n our inner city schools there has been a tendency to grading 'fours' for pupil capability because it was 'four' against national expectations. And certainly in the more advantaged schools there has been a tendency to over-grade. Trying to get subject inspectors to understand what you're saying is pretty hard!
>
> (RgI, Low Moors Secondary)

Corroboration

Several headteachers in our sample suspected that in some cases comments made by an individual teacher (or pupil) were often taken uncritically at face value by inspectors.

> Interviewing – I am more worried by this and I am not convinced of the objectivity. Things come through from teachers' 'flying kites' which are not necessarily checked out or set in a wider context. Some things were said in the report which indicate that the inspectors had been nobbled – the claim that middle management was over-burdened. Not sure of the body of evidence for this and it raises doubts about the impartiality of the process.
>
> (Deputy headteacher, Midchester Secondary)

Inspectors could also be aware of the problem.

> The intensity of activity in five days is so great that you have to respond to what you see at that point in time; you have to rely on staff comments saying, 'We have done this or that' or that 'this activity has taken place.'
>
> (Inspector, Alderman King Secondary)

Ideally, judgements should emerge from the corroboration of several sources of evidence. It may be argued that this occurs naturally as a consequence of the OFSTED methodology. For example, an inspector looking at mathematics will be expected to visit the classrooms of all teachers covering the pupil age and ability range. As already mentioned, each of these observations will be recorded on a LOF. In coming to a judgement on the overall quality of teaching the inspector will be able to consider perhaps a dozen or more descriptions of separate lessons. This will be assisted by the practice of aggregating grades across lessons so that, for example, a statement of the form 'In 80 per cent of the lessons observed teaching was sound or better' may be made. One chief inspector clearly saw the value of such aggregations:

> The force of the methodology comes through when the lesson gradings are aggregated. You reach a point in the week when you have a view of 80–100 observations and because they are quantified you can discern interesting trends. This is very powerful along with the views of the team coming at you. The balance between the quantitative data and what is seen gives a high level to the debate.
>
> (Chief Inspector, Foxton)

Another commented, 'I am not sure about the grading system – there is a danger of producing a norm referenced approach, so it doesn't prove anything. It is one of the weakest parts of HMI inspection . . . It can be spurious, although it sounds secure' (Chief Inspector, Stockpool).

Teacher disquiet about grading occasionally surfaced as well. 'I was amused but disappointed by the making of subjective judgements and then converting them into statistics,' one head of department told us. 'For example, 70 per cent of lessons were satisfactory – it is not clear what "satisfactory" means.[5] It gives an undeserved legitimacy to the whole exercise.'

Judgements made on a specific area of the curriculum are typically those of an individual inspector. Judgements on other aspects of a school, however, may not be the exclusive concern of a single inspector. Several, if not all inspectors are expected to contribute to judgements made on cross-curricular themes and other school-wide matters such as management. Problems can arise in these circumstances as indicated by the views of some of those involved in the inspection of Midchester Secondary:

> PSE [Personal and Social Education] took a hard knock – it relied on all the inspectors collating their views which is not a successful method of inspection.
>
> (Deputy headteacher)

> The [Information Technology] inspector wrote his piece on Wednesday before seeing what other people had said on this. It may be better to involve such inspectors in the inspection later in the week. A similar problem arose for the assessment section.
>
> (Inspection team leader)

> We didn't get to grips with management – the issues only became apparent during the inspection, we could have explored more. The question was posed when only the core team was left.
>
> (Inspector)

These last two concerns reflect the fact that in secondary school inspections subject specialist inspectors generally attend for just part of the inspection week. It is only the 'core' team which is involved for the whole week.

In emphasizing the importance of collective or consensus judgements the Handbook states: 'Reaching consensus about the quality of a school is most easily accomplished through discussion involving all team members towards the end of the inspection. If some members are unable to attend such a discussion, alternative ways of obtaining their views about the main findings will need to be established' (OFSTED 1994b: (3) 20), and again: 'Ensure that where more than one member has evidence on the same matter, the evidence is carefully collated, synthesized and evaluated' (OFSTED 1994b: (3)27).

Now, these injunctions are eminently sensible but they beg the question of how such operations are to be carried out. Reaching a 'true' consensus in meetings of a dozen or more individuals is neither easy nor are the strategies of doing so transparently obvious. Collation, synthesis and evaluation are deceptively straightforward terms which in practice refer to complex tasks of reducing and transforming what are essentially qualitative forms of data. The Handbook gives no guidance on the practice and procedures which lie behind these tasks.

Here are two RgIs reflecting on their experiences of coming to a collective judgement within the inspection team. The first describes how an issue related to gender was resolved:

> There was the example of where pupils were allowed to choose the groups in which they worked and on the whole boys worked with boys and girls worked with girls. Somebody said 'I think that is a real serious issue for the school'. Somebody else said, 'Why, what would you do in the situation?' 'Why exactly should boys and girls work together?' And then we got into a debate about styles of learning. The English inspector then said the way in which pupils interrogate text differs significantly between boys and girls. In the end that was the only point on which the two sides could agree ... [So] the compromise was that if there was something about the task itself which boys and girls would tackle differently then there was a legitimate reason for making them work together. If not, why should you be doing it?
>
> (RgI, Low Moors Secondary)

In general though the RgI thought that such occasions of real disagreement were rare. This was also the view of a second RgI who suggested that the JRS was the basic mechanism for expressing corporate judgement:

> People will argue their corner but it will usually only be between say a 'three' or a 'four', or a 'two' and a 'three'. It will only be a grade [difference on the JRS] ... The person responsible for an area leads on it. They come in with their examples but they don't come in with it written up usually. They've got their evidence in front of them, they talk about the evidence to show what they're going to give it on the whole and then you do your JRS against that.
>
> (RgI, Broad Lane Primary)

Judgements that are agreed between all (or at least a number of) inspectors are likely to be the most secure. This is perhaps reflected in the degree of confidence expressed by schools in judgements of different types. About two thirds of headteachers reported being satisfied with the overall quality of judgements made in the main findings of inspections. These are, in practice, the judgements which are most likely to have been agreed between several inspectors (OFSTED 1995b: 21). By contrast, only just over half of headteachers accepted the judgements made about particular subjects (the province, in the main, of individual inspectors).

Can validity be attested?

Sufficient has probably been said to see that potential threats to the validity of inspection judgements can arise in a number of ways. Given the very large number of judgements which are made during the course of inspection it is highly unlikely that all will be impeccable and above criticism. Individual inspections will therefore differ in the degree to which they can be regarded as valid.

The Handbook assumes that valid judgements arise in applying the relevant criteria. However, as noted above, making criteria explicit is no guarantee that they are internalized by inspectors and converted by some mental calculus into consistent judgements. To put the matter bluntly, we know little about how complex judgements are arrived at and even less about how inspectors actually deal with the numerous sets of criteria of which they are required to take account.

Now it might be argued that although there are very many specific judgements made during the course of an inspection, they are nevertheless consolidated into a limited number of 'key issues for action'. In doing so, any faulty judgements, if not too numerous, will be averaged out and thus not invalidate the main findings. Moreover, the main findings may be considered to be validated by the requirement that they should command the agreement of the inspection team. But just as little is known about what 'goes on' in the heads of individual inspectors so too there is a dearth of evidence about what goes on in groups of inspectors when they claim to have reached collective agreement.

The monitoring of inspections

OFSTED has a responsibility for monitoring the inspections which are carried out in its name. It does this in two ways. A sample of inspections are visited while in progress by individual HM Inspectors. Also at the end of every inspection a Record of Inspection Evidence (RoIE), together with the report and other relevant documentation, is forwarded to OFSTED. The RoIE is a detailed collection of the inspection findings much of which are summarized in terms of five- and seven-point scales.

In monitoring this substantial body of evidence OFSTED is mainly concerned to determine whether the judgements made in the report are consistent with the evidence contained in the RoIE. It is possible to track back in the documentation to show the extent to which judgements in the report relate to the various summaries of the RoIE and how these in turn derive from the individually completed forms (for lessons observed and other activities observed or carried out). Figure 6.1 provides a simple outline of what would be involved.

Starting with the report, an OFSTED 'monitor' would be able to check whether the main findings were consistent with the detailed findings dispersed throughout the text. The findings could then, in turn, be examined for consistency against what we term the 'second stage summaries' which consist largely of forms completed by individual inspectors. These summaries should also be consistent with the 'first stage summaries' which include the LOFs completed by each inspector.

It should be noted that these individual records cannot, in most cases, be compared directly to the 'individual inspection events' since the latter occurred as irretrievable happenings in the past (e.g observations of a particular lesson). As Maw rightly comments: 'There is no quantitative record of classroom events, there is no descriptive record either, nothing comparable to the ethnographer's

Figure 6.1 Schematic representation of our interpretation of the OFSTED inspection/reporting process

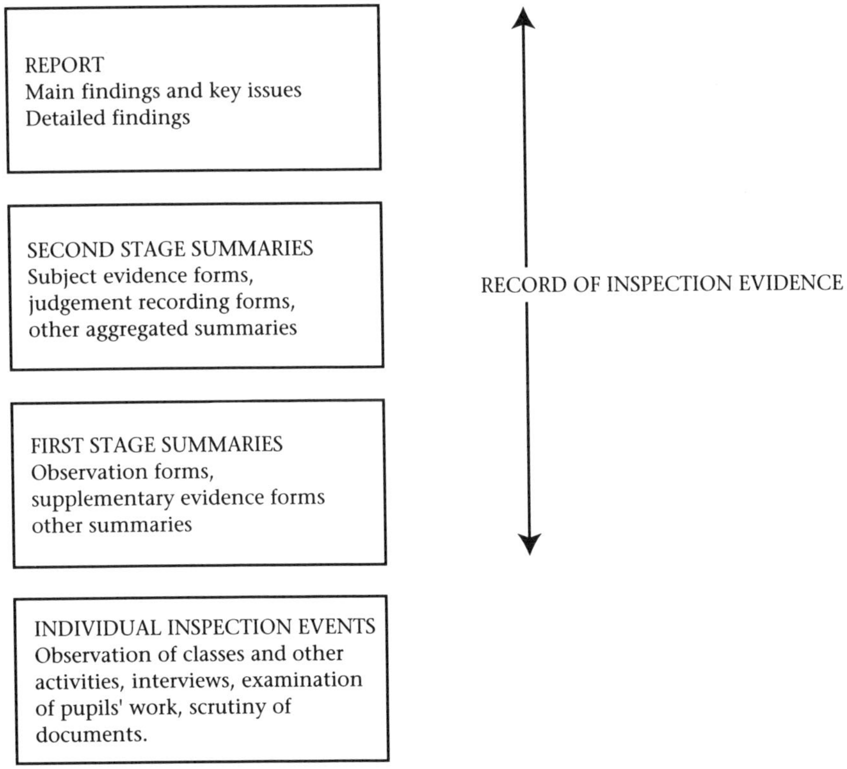

REPORT
Main findings and key issues
Detailed findings

SECOND STAGE SUMMARIES
Subject evidence forms,
judgement recording forms,
other aggregated summaries

RECORD OF INSPECTION EVIDENCE

FIRST STAGE SUMMARIES
Observation forms,
supplementary evidence forms
other summaries

INDIVIDUAL INSPECTION EVENTS
Observation of classes and other
activities, interviews, examination
of pupils' work, scrutiny of
documents.

notebook, for instance. *The only recorded outcome is, itself, evaluative'* (Maw 1995: 79; our emphasis). There can be no certainty about what processes were involved between the inspector experiencing an event and recording it on a LOF. At best it can only be assumed that the processes are guided by the criteria. Although the *consistency* of judgements within the RoIE may be demonstrated the question of *validity* remains indeterminate.

Although methods have been proposed for carrying out such 'audit trails' for checking the validity of qualitative investigations (see, for example, Lincoln and Guba 1985) they tend to be complex, lengthy and do not, as yet, command broad agreement. The extension of the audit trail to inspections is an interesting development. We do not know, however, in sufficient detail exactly how OFSTED carries out this task.

It might be argued that the validity of a report can be assessed by the degree to which those who 'know' the school, particularly the teachers, recognize and accept its findings. Indeed, it is not uncommon for headteachers to comment that the report describes the school as they know it to be. There are problems with this of course. A headteacher might be relieved to learn that inspectors had not uncovered the skeletons in the cupboard and be only too willing to agree with an overall favourable report. Then again the findings of reports can sometimes be fiercely contested by schools, particularly when the overall situation is described in very unfavourable terms. Contestation of a report may imply a lack of validity although not necessarily so.

The odds, of course, are stacked in favour of the inspectors, particularly under the arrangements of OFSTED inspections. For example, although the main findings of a report are discussed with the headteacher and other staff the opportunities for challenge are severely limited. 'Where there are errors of factual accuracy which have a significant bearing on the findings of an inspection, inspectors will make the necessary corrections and review the relevant judgements. Otherwise, there can be no modification of the judgements to be included in the report' (OFSTED 1994b: (2) 13).

In the end, it would seem that validity has to be taken on trust. We shall pursue this issue further from a more theoretical perspective in a later chapter. In the meantime, however, we take the claim of validity at face value and turn to a related matter. A valid inspection report contains *inter alia* a set of prescriptions (the 'key issues for action') for the further development of the school. In the chapter to follow we examine the extent of such post-inspection development and the conditions under which it occurs.

7 THE IMPACT OF INSPECTION ON SCHOOLS' DEVELOPMENT

The best laid schemes o' mice an' men
Gang aft a-gley
An' lea'e us nought but grief an' pain
For promis'd joy.

(Burns, To a Mouse)

What happens as a result of an inspection? Inspection is generally assumed by its advocates to lead to desirable change. Such an assumption is indeed an explicit aim of OFSTED inspections, as one HMCI made clear: 'I see the function of inspection as being . . . to present . . . findings in such a way that other schools may learn from a school's successes or that the school itself will be in no doubt where to concentrate its efforts in order to improve' (Sutherland 1992).

The relationship between inspection and school improvement is underlined in OFSTED's *Corporate Plan* which is subtitled 'Improvement through Inspection' (OFSTED 1993c). Inspection is also generally justified as an accountability mechanism; however, this need not necessarily be considered a distinctively different concern. Satisfying the demands of accountability presumably implies that some action (and thus change) should follow from the production of an account, especially if it contains elements of criticism. Wider claims for inspection have also been made which extend beyond the particular institution under review:

> It is sometimes assumed that 'improvement through inspection' is restricted to the school level; that OFSTED's impact, in other words, should be seen only in terms of its impact on the school inspected. This is clearly too limited and ignores the second important part of OFSTED's responsibility, which is to use the information collected through inspection to provide advice to the Secretary of State and draw attention to issues of educational concern.
>
> (Matthews and Smith 1995: 31)

Our concern here, however, is with the first of these two interpretations. The second lies outside of the scope of our empirical evidence.

How then can inspection lead to real change? We have already noted that changes can (and often do) result in the process of preparing for an inspection. School documentation may be brought up to date and in line with the expectations of inspectors. School premises may be smartened up in a variety of ways. Teachers are likely to attend more closely to the preparation of their lessons and the marking of homework, particularly during the actual inspection. We have also seen that inspection can give rise to additional stress and anxiety. Such effects, both positive and negative, are however likely to be relatively short-lived with 'normality' returning when the inspection is over.

Whether or not schools change as a consequence of an inspection rests on the extent to which the report is acted on. An inspection report typically formulates a set of general recommendations indicating how a school might address the specific weaknesses identified. In OFSTED inspections these recommendations are termed 'key issues for action' and are expected to be 'practicable, explicit and as few as are consistent with the inspection findings' (OFSTED 1994b: (2) 17). Such key issues or recommendations may be regarded as a skeletal outline for school change.

There is also a statutory requirement for the key issues to be incorporated within an 'action plan' (DFE 1993a). The action plan, therefore, represents a fleshing out of the outline and, ideally, a detailed strategy for future development.

We were especially interested in how schools responded to the recommendations made in relation to them. In particular, we wished to determine how and to what extent such recommendations were implemented in practice. From this perspective change was understood in terms of the degree of implementation achieved. We therefore followed up the inspections of all 24 schools in our case study sample (see Appendix). We did this by conducting individual semi-structured interviews in each school with, wherever possible, the same staff seen in the first phase of the research.[1] Interviews were also carried out with the school inspector responsible for liaising with the school.[2] Interviews, as before, lasted approximately 45 minutes each and were recorded.

Before coming to the issue of implementation we turn first to a more detailed acount of what was recommended.

A taxonomy of inspection recommendations

What did the inspectors recommend be done? The structure of their recommendations varied both within and across the reports. The majority took the form of short statements concerned with a single theme. Some, however, linked together two separate themes. In these cases the statements were divided into two so that each was regarded as a distinct recommendation. The number of recommendations varied from 4 to 11, with a total of 181 for all 24 inspections. The median number of recommendations (8.5) was somewhat higher than in subsequent OFSTED inspections where the norm has been around 5 (Northam 1993: 6).

A substantial proportion of the recommendations were elaborated in one of two ways. In the first case, brief details were given about how to carry out the recommendation. For example, a recommendation in the Low Springs report read: 'The school's 1992–1995 management plan should be reformulated to state targets more clearly and to develop action plans.' In the second case some kind of causal link was implied between different aspects of a recommendation. The report on Danbrook Primary, for example, stated: 'Curriculum discussion needs to take place in a systematic way involving the headteacher and senior management team in order to formulate and agree curriculum policies.'

Despite these differences in the internal structure of recommendations we concentrated our attention on what was considered to be the main focus, assigning each recommendation to one of several different categories. These categories represented major features of the curriculum, organization and management of schools. In cases where the main focus was not immediately apparent, reference to the context of the recommendation in the report usually clarified the situation.

In Table 7.1 the main recommendations have been grouped into 15 categories. Some differences in emphasis were apparent between secondary and primary inspections. For example, recommendations concerned with teaching and learning were a more frequent outcome of secondary inspections. Over one in five fell into this category; for example: 'The school should plan and carry out a staff development programme to enable all staff to deliver an appropriate range of teaching and learning styles to meet the needs of all pupils' (Carlow Secondary). For the primary schools the most frequently occurring recommendations were those involved with aspects of:

- Management/administration

  The school should draw up job descriptions which describe more precisely teachers' responsibilities and duties.

  (Low Springs Primary)

- School development planning

  The headteacher and staff, with the support of the governing body, should review the school development plan to identify clear priorities, clarify staff

Table 7.1 Types of recommendations made in primary and secondary inspections

Recommendation type	Primary inspections (n = 13) % of recommendations*	Secondary inspections (n = 11) % of recommendations*
Assessment	11	9
Curriculum delivery	10	15
Curriculum documentation	13	8
Curriculum monitoring and evaluation	6	5
Curriculum (specific)	14	5
Organization	2	6
School development planning	12	5
Environment/accommodation	3	7
Equal opportunities	2	3
Links outside	0	3
Management/administration	15	8
Pastoral/discipline	0	3
Special educational needs	2	1
Teaching and learning	5	20
Resources	4	2
Number of recommendations	93	88

*Percentages are obtained by rounding up.

responsibilities and allocate resources appropriately in order to achieve the school's objectives.

(Richardson Primary)

• Curriculum (specific)

A planned programme of provision in history and geography should be developed to ensure coverage of the programmes of study.

(Milton Primary)

Amongst the most frequently occurring categories in both primary and secondary inspections were those concerned with:

• Assessment

Implement the whole school policy for assessment, recording and reporting especially as it relates to the National Curriculum.

(Midchester Secondary)

• Curriculum delivery

In a number of areas of the curriculum statutory requirements are not being met fully. The school needs to ensure that all areas of the National Curriculum are covered.

(Alderman King Secondary)

• Curriculum documentation

Policy statements for all core and foundation subjects should be produced as soon as possible.

(St Peter's Junior)

Overall about half of the recommendations were concerned with the curriculum and assessment, seen very much as a nationally prescribed product to be delivered through the agency of an explicit management system. The system was one in which precise documentation, planning and procedures were of central significance. In addition, the importance of regular curriculum monitoring and evaluation was emphasized in a number of inspections:

Senior and middle management should be more consistently involved in monitoring various aspects of curriculum planning and implementation.

(Potterton Secondary)

The embodiment of this approach is apparent in the current preoccupation with school development plans (SDPs). This notion has been vigorously promoted by the government and LEAs and supported by an influential body of related educational writing (Caldwell and Spinks 1988, 1992; Hargreaves and Hopkins 1991). Perhaps more than any other aspect of school organization the possession of an appropriately constructed SDP has become the *sine qua non* of the 'good school'. Recommendations concerned with establishing structures of organization may also be seen as consistent with the emphasis on management and planning:

The school should establish a whole-school policy steering group and associated cross-curricular working parties.

(Carlow Secondary)

Apart from teaching and learning the remaining recommendations were distributed amongst a relatively diverse set of concerns: environment/accommodation; resources; equal opportunities; links outside; pastoral/discipline; and special educational needs.

Although the recommendations for the majority of our inspections related to whole-school issues some, as we have already noted, were directed at specific areas of the curriculum. In addition, the recommendations arising from each of the three Sedley 'supported self-evaluations' were concerned exclusively with a specific area of the curriculum: language in the case of Fenby Junior; reading for Lowstone Primary; and mathematics in Turner Secondary. Although all of these recommendations fell under the category of *curriculum (specific)* they were further analysed using the full range of the taxonomy. We have subsequently found that the taxonomy is sufficiently comprehensive for analysing both whole-school 'key issues' and the more specific recommendations dispersed throughout the text of OFSTED reports.

The implementation of recommendations

Studies of school improvement have usually relied on participants' accounts to establish the extent to which changes had been implemented. In the absence of any practical alternatives we did the same. We asked our interviewees to describe the action(s) which had been taken on each of the recommendations arising from their inspection. This was supplemented with a rating for each on a scale of 'implementation'. The interviews took place approximately nine months after the inspection.[3]

Interviewees were also requested to identify any influences which they considered significant in either facilitating or inhibiting the implementation of each recommendation. At the same time, views were sought on whether there had been any other significant outcomes of inspection (whether beneficial or otherwise) and the nature of any post-inspection support from the LEA.

When the implementation ratings and descriptions for each recommendation were examined we found a good degree of consensus amongst teachers and inspectors. For some recommendations, however, rating and description differences were apparent. There are several possible reasons for such discrepancies. Headteachers may have tended to give more favourable ratings than their staff. Teachers may have had a partial view of school-wide implementation and really only known how recommendations had affected their own class or curriculum area. The school inspectors also admitted that they had insufficient knowledge of how things had progressed in many cases since the inspection. This lack of complete consensus struck us as the way things were 'on the ground'. Several perspectives on implementation can be legitimately held within the same institution. We suspect, as well, that interviewees probably gave themselves and their institutions the benefit of the doubt when deciding whether implementation had actually occurred; our picture may err on the optimistic side.

In such circumstances we looked particularly closely for consistency and corroboration amongst the descriptions given of the form that implementation had actually taken. As a result we felt more confident about assigning an overall rating on a (slightly modified) implementation scale covering the range: full implementation; substantial implementation; some implementation; limited implementation; no implementation. The results of applying the scale are summarized in Table 7.2.

Table 7.2 Extent of implementation of recommendations from secondary (n = 11) and primary (n = 13) inspections

	Extent of implementation					
	Full	Substantial	Some	Limited	None	Total
Number	20	21	70	31	39	181
% of total	11	12	39	17	22	101*

* Percentages are obtained by rounding up.

Table 7.3 Extent of implementation of recommendations from secondary inspections (n = 11) only (a) about 9 months after inspection and (b) about 21 months after inspection

	Extent of implementation					
	Full	Substantial	Some	Limited	None	Total
After 9 months	10 (11%)	10 (11%)	33 (38%)	14 (16%)	21 (24%)	88 (100%)
After 21 months	17 (19%)	16 (18%)	34 (39%)	9 (10%)	12 (14%)	88 (100%)

As can be seen, across all 24 cases, only 11 per cent of the recommendations could be considered 'fully' implemented nine months or so after the inspection. A further 12 per cent fell in the 'substantially implemented' category. Nearly 40 per cent of recommendations, however, were either unimplemented (22 per cent) or implemented only to a 'limited' extent (17 per cent). A comparable proportion of recommendations were classified as having undergone 'some' implementation.

In the case of the secondary inspections it was possible to carry out a further round of interviews up to a year later, or some 18–21 months after the original inspections. Table 7.3 brings together details of the extent of implementation for the secondary inspections at the nine-month and 21-month periods respectively.

Some improvement in implementation is evident. The proportion of recommendations fully or substantially implemented rose from 22 per cent to 37 per cent. The proportion characterized by limited or no implementation fell from 40 per cent to 24 per cent. Those recommendations where only partial implementation had occurred remained much the same (just under 40 per cent).

Further analysis of the data indicated that some recommendation types were more difficult to implement than others. For example, it is significant that none of the recommendations relating specifically to teaching and learning were fully or substantially implemented by the time of our first interviews. A year later when we again visited the secondary schools only 17 per cent reached this highest level of implementation (table not shown). Recommendations concerned with curriculum delivery also had low levels of implementation with only about one in seven being at least substantially implemented after 21 months or so.

Implementation in these areas is likely to be most difficult since they often require wholesale changes in the behaviours of teachers and pupils. Other recommendation types such as those focusing on the production of planning and curriculum documentation are likely to be more frequently implemented.

Variation across individual inspections

How far did schools' experiences conform to the general patterns? When implementation was viewed in terms of individual inspections a diverse pattern was again apparent (see Table 7.4). A number of inspections were found to have very low levels of implementation and correspondingly high levels of non-implementation at the time of the follow-up interviews. The most extreme examples were: Milton Primary where nothing had been fully or substantially implemented nine months later; Austin Road Primary; Alderman King Secondary; and Carlow Secondary. By contrast, a few schools were characterized by high implementation and low non-implementation – Murbank Primary where almost half the recommendations had been fully or substantially implemented; Trenton Storrs Middle; and Ecclesley Secondary.

In the second round of interviews (involving the secondary schools only) levels of implementation generally increased although several schools (Laurels, Alderman King, Potterton, Monkton and Turner) still had about a half of their recommendations largely unimplemented. Ecclesley tended to re-assess the

Table 7.4 Implementation of inspection report recommendations by school

	Percentage of recommendations implemented			
	9 months after			
Primary schools inspected	*Full + substantial*	*Limited + none*		
Richardson Primary	25	25		
Murbank Primary	44	0		
Playfair Primary	13	38		
St Peter's Junior	10	60		
Low Springs Primary	18	45		
Milton Primary	0	55		
Austin Road Primary	0	57		
St Mark's Middle	20	40		
Trenton Storrs Middle	33	0		
High Lees Primary	11	44		
Danbrook Primary	20	20		
Fenby Junior	50	50		
Lowstone Primary	22	56		
	9 months after		*21 months after*	
Secondary schools inspected	*Full + substantial*	*Limited + none*	*Full + substantial*	*Limited + none*
Ecclesley Secondary	88	0	63	0
Prince Edward Secondary	30	20	50	10
Laurels Secondary	11	33	44	44
Midchester Secondary	17	0	33	0
Alderman King Secondary	0	60	20	40
Potterton Secondary	20	40	20	40
Monkton Secondary	29	43	14	57
Carlow Secondary	0	81	27	27
Strafford Secondary	40	40	60	10
Tennyson Road Secondary	0	0	50	0
Turner Secondary	9	73	18	54

extent of implementation it had secured in a downward direction the second time around although it continued to remain the 'best' post-inspection performer.

These levels of implementation need to be interpreted with caution, not least because the aggregation process involved assumes that recommendations are of equal importance. This is certainly not the case as will soon become clear. One needs to look behind these figures at what actually took place. Four schools are therefore examined in rather more detail.

We have chosen Murbank, Milton, Ecclesley and Alderman King schools. The first two are examples of primary inspections where concern had been expressed about the quality of the education provided. The level of concern was greater in Murbank which was considered to be 'at risk' (see earlier). The identification of such schools is a priority of OFSTED inspections and at the heart of the current political debate about education.

The other two schools are representative, in their differing ways, of schools judged to be providing a broadly satisfactory standard of education. They were schools, in other words, with undeniable strengths but which nevertheless had areas where improvement was possible. Schools of this latter kind constitute the majority of our sample as they do across the country as a whole.

Four case studies of implementation

Murbank Primary: crucial support from the school inspector

Murbank Primary was a school considered to be providing an unsatisfactory level of education with widespread underachievement in all of the core and most of the foundation subjects. These deficiencies were attributed to: the lack of whole-school planning policies and schemes of work; poor management of the curriculum, staff and resources; and low teacher expectations of pupils. Seven of the nine recommendations for action were related directly to these aspects.

Whole-school planning was to be addressed by formulating a more systematic school development plan and by reviewing 'directed time' so as to allow teachers more opportunity for planning and for curriculum development. At the time of our interviews both of these two recommendations had been at least substantially implemented.

Improved curriculum management and planning was to be accomplished by: reviewing the timetable in order to reduce the amount of 'unproductive' non-curriculum time; revising the statement of school aims to give greater emphasis to academic achievement; and developing schemes of work in line with the National Curriculum to include guidance on differentiation and teaching strategies. The first of these recommendations had been substantially implemented. Less progress had, however, been made on the other two. Although the school aims had been adjusted it was generally felt that their realization in terms of classroom practice would be a slower process. Progress had been made in developing schemes of work for the core subjects and those for the foundation subjects were to follow in due course.

Two recommendations were concerned with resource management. An audit of resources was well on the way to completion and some progress had been made on developing a prioritized curriculum budget alongside the school development plan. The remaining two recommendations were related to improving the internal environment of the school by rectifying certain Health and Safety contraventions and redecorating parts of the school. Work had been undertaken on both of these.

In other words, at the time of our interviews, approximately nine months after the inspection, the school had made serious efforts to tackle all the recommendations, had generally implemented four and was making good progress on the remainder.

As we noted earlier the main influences on the post-inspection phase had been the interest and commitment of governors, the efforts of the teachers particularly during the holidays, improved organization of staff and team meetings and, most of all, the extended involvement of the school inspector. The main negative influence was reflected in the complaint about lack of time. However, when re-inspection occurred a year or so after the original inspection it was apparent that the school was still causing concern. How was it then after such a promising post-inspection phase that improvement had been so short-lived? In the inspectors' view the headteacher had been unable to sustain the initiative once the school inspector had had to withdraw from active involvement and day-to-day support.

It should also be noted that the underlying malaise of the school was rooted in a situation of profound underachievement and low expectations. The implicit strategy in the recommendations proposed was to address the situation *indirectly* through management and planning processes and procedures. It is significant that the only two recommendations where the central issue of teaching and learning was specifically identified were amongst the three where only some degree of implementation had occurred.

Murbank's experiences would suggest that producing discernible improvements in pupils' learning and achievements is likely to be a much slower and more uncertain process than changing planning and management procedures.

Milton Primary: an unconvinced headteacher

Unlike Murbank, Milton is a small village primary school drawing on a relatively advantaged catchment. Although the school was clearly not in the 'at risk' category the inspectors were, nonetheless, concerned about a number of things: the provision of the National Curriculum, the curriculum management responsibilities of the headteacher, and the relationships between the school and its parents and governors.

Of the nine recommendations proposed for action three were concerned with the development and delivery of specific aspects of the curriculum (English, mathematics, history and geography). Progress was proceeding on all of these but English. The headteacher disagreed with the recommendation concerning English and firmly believed that the school's existing provision covered all the points raised by the inspectors. Some progress was underway in the other areas – most so in mathematics where a review had been conducted which would in turn lead to the adoption of a new scheme.

The inspectors also emphasized the importance of explicit policy documents for both the curriculum and pupil assessment/recording. Some implementation of the latter had occurred, helped by involvement in work with neighbouring schools on the development of assessment booklets. The headteacher was, however, less convinced of the need for detailed policy documents for the curriculum.

The headteacher disagreed with the inspectors' emphasis on establishing a system for monitoring and evaluating the curriculum. This was already felt to be in place and, as a result, no serious attempt had been made to implement a new approach. The suggestion that the headteacher himself should undertake classroom monitoring of the curriculum was not considered feasible because heavy involvement in 'local management' issues made 'getting round classrooms' much more difficult.

The headteacher had also been urged to develop a more structured approach to management planning by involving staff in the process. Some meetings had taken place and the school development plan was in the process of being reworked. Finally a start had been made on reviewing the methods used in communicating with parents and governors.

Overall, then, limited progress had been made in implementing the report's recommendations in the nine months or so following the inspection. Governors, particularly those who were newly appointed, were seen as being a significant spur to such action as had occurred. Issues about the inspection report had been raised by parents and a few had withdrawn their children from the school. There was, in the words of the school inspector, 'still a lot of turmoil about'.

The inspectors saw a need for a refocusing of the headteacher's role. The balance of responsibility between the headteacher (towards organization) and the deputy (towards the curriculum) had led to the headteacher's marginalization from the curriculum. With the imminent departure of the deputy (through promotion) it was thought essential that the headteacher filled the resulting vacuum and re-exerted curriculum leadership.

In retrospect the inspectors felt they had 'back-pedalled' somewhat from being critical of the headteacher. Had they not done so the LEA's formal post-inspection monitoring system would have been triggered. However, the school inspector had been given an additional two extra days to expedite progress in the school.

Ecclesley Secondary – limits imposed by the pupil intake[4]

This school and the one to follow are drawn from our secondary sample. The accounts are based on our second set of follow-up interviews.

Ecclesley is an 11–16 secondary school set in an urban area of substantial social disadvantage. The inspectors who knew the school beforehand spoke of it as 'a school we were proud of' and where 'the management was particularly good'. The bulk of the inspection recommendations were concerned with aspects of curriculum provision and policy development. A couple of administratively-oriented recommendations were also proposed: an extension to the school day; and the need to ensure greater pupil access to the school libraries.

All of the recommendations were seriously tackled with five out of the total of eight being fully or substantially implemented. In addition, satisfactory progress was being made in addressing the remaining three.

The recommendation on which there was least progress was one concerned with matching provision more closely to the needs of pupils, particularly the boys. Factors which were thought by members of the school to have an adverse effect on this included: the generally low level of literacy and oracy of many pupils on entry; the wide range of ability which made the kinds of differentiation advocated by the inspectors difficult to achieve; and lack of motivation to succeed in school in an area of high unemployment. These factors were believed to apply particularly to boys who were also affected adversely by the macho culture of the former mining area in which Ecclesley was set.

The school had been dealing with these problems in several ways – mainly by tackling them for pupils of both sexes, not just for the boys. A corrective reading programme had been introduced before the inspection which involved the withdrawal of pupils from their English lessons. The inspectors considered that the programme restricted access to the National Curriculum. The school's view was that pupils could not benefit from the curriculum unless they could read. This was a potential source of conflict and, though the school had made some changes, it was made clear that the programme would not be abandoned.

As far as the boys were concerned, staff were at a loss to solve what was felt to be a national problem. It was being tackled by the introduction of a scheme whereby the top 40 per cent of children would be closely monitored and given individual help where necessary.

The school's well-regarded senior management team had been a major influence on the level of implementation achieved. They had taken the initiative in setting up appropriate structures (working parties and a middle management forum) to tackle the recommendations. They were also involved in monitoring the developments, although time pressures were reported as a major constraint.

Alderman King: a question of priorities and uncertainties

Alderman King is a medium size 11–18 comprehensive school situated in a small town which draws pupils from a mix of socio-economic backgrounds. The inspectors' report suggested a school which was committed to a consultative style of leadership and where the standards achieved were generally satisfactory.

The report identified five recommendations. After a period of 18 months or so the overall level of implementation achieved, however, was at best modest. Only one recommendation had been substantially implemented and the others were described as having undergone some or limited implementation.

Limited progress had been made in the provision of a special needs programme for individual departments and pupils. The main problem was that the SEN coordinator was perceived as 'not being really up to the job'. The senior management had attempted to develop the role of the coordinator through membership of the Key Stage 3 management team. Although the profile of special needs had been raised it was felt that the coordinator was still lacking in 'proaction'. As a result teachers felt that there had been little improvement in in-class support.

Progress had also been slow in clarifying staff roles through the production of detailed job descriptions. This was seen as a major task for the hard-pressed senior management team which had been somewhat disrupted by the second-ment of one of the deputies. The headteacher wanted this recommendation to be phased in with the appraisal process which was underway. As a result implementation was seen as a matter of timing. Some discussions had taken place with a few staff but job descriptions had not yet been committed to paper.

Some progress had been made in seeking to meet the need to increase pupils' motivation and levels of challenge. Staff awareness of the issues was addressed through in-school INSET to which inspectors had contributed. One innovation had been the introduction of a 'curriculum enrichment' programme for Year 7/Year 8 pupils. It was thought that such developments as had occurred were due more to the school's involvement in TVEI and, more recently, GNVQ-related developments than to the recommendation itself.

The inspectors reported that the school was not meeting statutory National Curriculum requirements in some areas. The headteacher felt that this recom-mendation was vague and was not clear which departments were considered at fault. The deputy was only aware of one department for which the criticism was appropriate. The deputy was also not sure how to check the other depart-ments and therefore relied on the professionalism of the heads of department for information. The head stressed the uncertainty associated with the National Curriculum in the light of the impending Dearing review[5] and felt justified 'in protecting staff from chasing false hares'.

The one recommendation which had been substantially implemented referred to the need for a more developed school plan to include targets, staff responsibilities and so on. The plan had been refined and updated with greater involvement of staff than previously, although one head of department con-sidered that it still lacked clear objectives and time-lines. It was confidently expected that the school development plan would be in place for the next school year.

The four case studies reveal *inter alia* some of the factors, both internal and external to the school, which were influential in the implementation process. In the following section we examine the pattern of influences across all 24 cases with a view to relating them to the broader phenomenon of educational change.

Overview of influences

The pattern of influences across all 24 inspections is summarized in Table 7.5. This shows the 'top' (most frequently cited) five or so categories of influence separately for primary and secondary inspections, according to whether they were positive (helped implementation) or negative (hindered implementation).

Table 7.5 also shows the pattern nine or so months after inspection and again, in the case of secondary schools only, 18 or more months on. As can be seen some influences can operate, according to circumstances, either positively or negatively. These include: the qualities of the *headteacher and/or SMT* (as in the Ecclesley and Milton cases) and also those of *teachers* (as at Murbank and Alderman King).

Other potentially bi-polar influences frequently identified were *funding* and *staffing*. The lack of funding was very apparent in the inspection of Prince Edward Secondary. There the library was seen as a major way of addressing the recommendation of 'develop[ing] clear strategies for resourcing the learning process'. Although much had been done since the inspection to develop the library as a multi-resource area, lack of funds was seen as the principal constraint. On the positive side the provision of funding through the LEA's capital programme had enabled the school to tackle 'the isolated and delapidated nature of music, art and home economics accommodation'.

Where staffing appeared as a positive influence it tended to be associated with opportunities for making new appointments, promoting staff, and creating new staffing structures. Where cited as a negative influence this generally referred to weaknesses in the existing staffing structure. For example, in Potterton Secondary a structure based on small departments resulted in heads of department being over-burdened and thus less able to carry out the kind of monitoring functions envisaged by the inspectors.

The creation of appropriate *organizational groups* was sometimes seen as crucial as in Ecclesley Secondary or, again, in Danbrook Primary where a new headteacher was able to establish a structure of regular staff meetings where

Table 7.5 Most frequently reported influences on implementation 9–12 months and 18–21 months after inspection

Primary 9–12 months after inspection	Secondary 9–12 months after inspection	Secondary 18–21 months after inspection
Positive influences		
Funding (11)	Teachers (13)	Staffing (13)
Teachers (8)	Staffing (11)	HT/SMT (11)
Materials/equipment (8)	HT/SMT (8)	Other non-local initiatives (11)
Staffing (8)	Funding (8)	Inspection itself (8)
Organizational groups (8)	Organizational groups (8)	
Negative influences		
Time (20)	National curriculum (20)	Time (13)
Teachers (14)	Time (13)	Teachers (11)
Funding (11)	Staffing (10)	Staffing (10)
Staffing (11)	Funding (10)	HT/SMT (7)
HT/SMT (9)	Teachers (10)	Funding (7)

Note: Figures in parentheses represent the percentage of all implementation categories across all inspections for each sector (primary, secondary) separately.

there had been little previous tradition of staff involvement in planning and development.

Non-local initiatives affecting secondary schools at the same time as inspection could sometimes provide additional momentum for implementation. This was apparent in some of the secondary inspections where external projects such as TVEI and GNVQ resulted in outcomes and activities consistent with inspection recommendations.

The *inspection process* itself was also viewed as a catalyst, especially where the proposed changes had been previously mooted. Although in general *inspectors* were not cited very frequently, where they were, the reference was invariably positive. In the case of Murbank the school inspector was regarded as *the* major influence on implementation.

Top of the list of negative influences on the secondary inspections was the *National Curriculum*. Continual changes in the requirements for the National Curriculum were seen as a major inhibitor of curriculum-related recommendations in several schools. In most cases schools were awaiting the changes to emerge from the Dearing Review (SCAA 1994), which had begun its deliberations soon after the inspections. As a result they were tending to defer implementation. As one head of department put it, 'You don't spend half your time putting fancy painting on a coffin!' For inspections generally however, it was *time*, or the lack of it, that was most frequently cited as the factor that militated against carrying out tasks to ensure implementation.

Other inspection outcomes and post-inspection support

Recommendations represent the formal expression of what inspectors hope will be the ultimate outcome of the inspection process. Our interviewees often identified other outcomes which were considered significant although not mentioned as recommendations or in the report.

Incidental changes in school management and organization occurred after a number of inspections. For example, the headteacher of Low Springs had felt it necessary to review procedures for relating to parents and children at playtime. Generalized effects of inspection on the teachers could result in a sharpening of their thinking and improvement in attitudes and morale.

Headteachers and senior staff tended to see the recommendations as a support for their existing ideas and desire for change. It sometimes appeared as though inspection had added an authority and legitimacy to such agendas.

Negative outcomes were also sometimes identified. In Low Springs, for example, fewer trips were now organized for pupils. This was a consequence of learning from the inspection of parental complaints about costs. At Murbank teachers were feeling the consequences; some had unsuccessfully applied for posts elsewhere and were worried whether being at the school was proving to be a disadvantage. The school inspector was aware of this issue and had sought to reassure staff that 'their careers were not doomed'.

Almost all schools indicated they had received some support, mainly through contact maintained by the school inspector. Other specialist inspectors and advisory staff were also mentioned by some schools. Generally, though, the extent of post-inspection support by LEAs was limited. This was attributed to the expanding programme of inspections which left the inspectors with little opportunity for follow-up work in the schools.

Implementation: overview and interpretation

The inspections studied in our research represent a sample of schools, probably similar to many throughout the country, which were still coming to terms with the profound educational changes initiated by government policy in recent years. In essence these changes constituted a significant reconceptualization of the curriculum as a nationally-prescribed product to be 'delivered' through the agency of an explicit management system.

This bias towards the concerns of management rather than pedagogy is reflected in the pattern of recommendation types identified. For example, recommendations *directly* concerned with teaching and learning, the defining purpose of schools, formed a relatively modest proportion of the total of all recommendation types (see Table 7.1). The majority of recommendations dealt with what were considered to be the necessary management conditions for effective teaching and learning – explicit documentation, detailed procedures and rational planning approaches.

Our data suggest that the extent to which schools were able to respond effectively to the findings of inspection was likely to be somewhat uncertain. Up to a year after inspection the pattern of implementation for all types of inspection was patchy. Only about a quarter or so of the recommendations could be said to be at least substantially implemented and nearly 40 per cent remained essentially unimplemented. After a further six to nine months there was some additional, albeit modest, improvement. It may be that the rate of implementation begins to decline with time. If so, the full implementation of recommendations may be a protracted process – if, indeed, it is completed at all.

There were indications that some types of recommendation were more likely to be implemented than others. There may be several reasons for this variation. Occasionally a headteacher was unconvinced of the validity or urgency of some of the recommendations. In such cases the fact of little or no response was not surprising. In the majority of cases, however, there was little evidence of such overt blocking. Most recommendations were treated seriously and differences were more likely to be the result of some recommendations being intrinsically easier to accomplish than others. For example, in the Low Springs inspection it was no doubt easier to 'provide curriculum information to governors' than to devise a 'system of evaluating school practices and policies'. Furthermore, recommendations which implicitly assume some consequent change in the practice of teachers (often, by implication, all teachers) are likely to be among the most difficult to accomplish in the short term.

In other words some recommendations, such as those involved in changing the pedagogical skills of teachers, represent major change programmes in their own right. Simply altering what may be regarded as the management 'externals' of documentation, procedures and systems is unlikely to lead to immediate changes at the level of the individual classroom.

The resources to which a school has access – particularly in terms of the skills of its staff – are likely to be of paramount importance. If these are not appropriate and readily available then successful implementation may be delayed or even not occur at all. The efforts of the headteacher and senior staff can be crucial here.

Over and above the specific characteristics of individual recommendations it was apparent that certain features within the context of schools could also exert an influence on implementation. The problem of insufficient time, for example, was mentioned by at least some staff in all inspections. Some prioritization is therefore both a realistic and a natural response. This fact is explicitly recognized by OFSTED in its interim guidance to inspectors pending the adoption of a further revision of the Framework and Handbook in 1996: 'The [key] issues should be given in order of priority which reflects their importance in improving the educational standards of the school. The order may be discussed with the school before being finalized' (OFSTED 1995a: 27).

Inspection and Fullan's model of school improvement

In the literature on school improvement, which has burgeoned over the last 30 or so years, little attention has been paid to the role that inspection might play in the process of change. This is partly because inspection has been absent from the portfolio of evaluation activities in many countries. But it is also partly because the inspection of schools has not, hitherto, been envisaged on the scale currently underway.

Michael Fullan (1982; 1991) has developed one of the most comprehensive accounts to date of the processes of educational change. In this final section we draw on his work for two reasons. First, because it is one of the most influential and widely read sources of advice to practitioners about how to bring about educational change, particularly in its recent, more popular forms (see Fullan 1992; Fullan and Hargreaves 1992). And second, because we were particularly concerned to see whether, in the absence of strongly formed 'theories' about how inspection works, there were clear parallels with other strategies for inducing change in schools.

The first set of key factors Fullan identifies relates to the nature of the proposed changes; he terms these the *characteristics of change*. They include the perceived 'need' for the changes, their potential 'complexity', their 'clarity', and their 'quality/practicality'.

At a superficial level the 'need' for the changes identified in the inspections we studied was recognized by most of those interviewed. Even the staff of Murbank Primary, who were initially most perturbed by the generally negative evaluation of their performance, came to terms with the need for change. Perceptions of the extent to which there was 'a need for change' varied, however, within schools. As our data suggest there were several occasions when the reports were seen to have legitimated senior staff agendas for change at the expense of other views. Such differences in perception affected implementation and could be picked up even a year or so later.

The extent to which recommendations had been implemented was clearly affected by their 'complexity'. In all schools a clear pattern had emerged. Curriculum documentation, for example, had been revised and updated but progress on changing teaching and learning styles had proved more intractable.

The 'clarity' of a report's recommendations was not always evident. Headteachers and staff commented that sometimes they were not sure what inspectors *really* had in mind in proposing a particular recommendation. In a few cases they also felt that the inspectors' own understanding of a situation, leading to the formulation of a recommendation, had been unclear.

There were a few intimations of staff doubts about the 'quality/practicality' of proposed changes that did not take account of what were considered significant external limitations. For example, the implementation of assessment policies and schemes of work could not, in the short term, be assumed straightforward, given the uncertainty about national assessments and definitive curriculum orders that then existed.

Recognition that the formulation of recommendations alone may not necessarily constitute a clear programme for change is apparent in the OFSTED requirement that a school produce a detailed action plan in which targets and responsibilities are specified. Even an action plan, however, may not be enough to generate real commitment unless it can also be expressed as a worthy vision for those involved. Securing this is likely to be a highly demanding and creative task. Although there were some indications that headteachers saw inspection recommendations as a means of furthering their own aspirations for their schools, we found little evidence of any developed strategies to ensure wide ownership of the process of change. To neglect this aspect is to run the risk of implementation being seen simply as a crude exercise of power legitimation on the part of the headteacher; superficial compliance rather than genuine commitment to change is the likely outcome.

In the inspections we studied we saw little indication of headteachers having turned the inspection recommendations into broader visions and strategies that were owned by the staff. Action plans were by no means inspiring documents and subsequent implementation was essentially seen as a mundane process.

The second group of factors to which Fullan refers are what he terms *local characteristics*. These include factors associated with the headteacher, teaching staff and governing body. Such factors, especially the first two, were discernible in our analysis. Also noteworthy was the extent to which LEA inspectors and advisory staff could be influential in promoting and securing change, despite the difficulties under which they were working.

Fullan groups a variety of influences under his third heading of *external factors* operating beyond the school and the LEA. In our study the earlier inspections arose in part as a consequence of LEAs' response to government exhortations to develop systems for monitoring and evaluating schools, and could be said to represent some kind of mandate beyond the LEA. Under the OFSTED arrangements this kind of pressure has been strengthened because inspections are mandatory. The publication of inspection reports, and the requirement for action plans, will doubtless help to ensure that follow-up of reports is taken seriously by schools.

Fullan (1991: 91) maintains that successful innovation includes elements of both *pressure* and *support*. This is likely to apply to inspection-induced change as well. These elements were particularly clear in the inspection of Murbank Primary, where pressure was provided by the governors, by the LEA, and by the prospect of re-inspection whilst support was also offered through the LEA's inspectorate.

Implementation for most changes, Fullan holds, takes two or more years. Our finding therefore that the implementation of inspection report recommendations is far from complete even after 18 months or so is consistent with Fullan's estimate. Fullan also identifies two phases beyond implementation. *Institutionalization* means changes being sustained beyond the first year or so of implementation and becoming an ongoing part of the system. According to Fullan, institutionalization of an innovation can typically take from three to five years to accomplish after its initial adoption. If a similar time scale holds for inspection-induced changes then the maintenance of teachers' long-term commitment to them may be difficult to secure. At the same time, in the current climate, schools may experience problems in maintaining the momentum to tackle recommendations as new pressures emerge. If quick implementation is not achieved, schools may be tempted to discontinue their efforts in order to respond to the latest demands.

Ultimately, of course, the hope is that implementation and institutionalization will lead to improvements in the quality of education on offer and the learning achieved by pupils. This corresponds to Fullan's second post-implementation phase of *outcome*. We have already noted that relatively few of the total number of recommendations were concerned directly with teaching and learning. The majority were related to the more general processes of curriculum delivery and management. The assumption here would seem to be that such processes, if implemented, constitute necessary if not sufficient conditions for changes at the classroom level. Significant changes in pupils' learning are therefore likely to be apparent only at the stage of institutionalization or beyond. Certainly none of the schools, within the time-scale of our study, was able to cite any evidence meeting this acid test of improvement.[6]

8 INSPECTION AND THE CASE OF THE 'FAILING' SCHOOL

It is not enough to succeed. Others must fail.

(Vidal)

When HMI's reports were first published in the early 1980s the examples which caught the public's attention were the schools in trouble. Reports on schools such as the Liverpool Institute for Boys (which numbered some of the Beatles amongst its former pupils) and Madeley Court (in relation to which the inspectors declared that 'caring was not enough') were the subject of press furore. They were joined in the late 1980s by Hackney Free and Parochial Church of England School. Such instances, however, were seen as exceptional cases. Following the 1992 and 1993 Education Acts the identification of 'failing schools' became a statutory requirement of inspections.[1] Indeed, OFSTED has subsequently made a special point of focusing much of its public presentation on such institutions and their improvement.

Registered inspectors have the responsibility for deciding whether a school is 'failing', or is likely to fail, to provide an acceptable standard of education. In coming to that decision consideration has to be given to the extent to which serious weaknesses are present in any or all of the following areas:

- the educational standards achieved
- the quality of education provided
- the pupils' spiritual, moral, social and cultural development
- the management and efficiency of the school.

Consideration must be given to the combined weight of such factors in reaching the final judgement. This is communicated by the RgI to the headteacher and then to OFSTED. A draft report is submitted to HMCI. If HMCI agrees with the RgI's judgement the school will be subject to 'special measures'. If HMCI does not agree, then the draft report will be appropriately amended. Failing schools are required to demonstrate improvement through the implementation of an action plan after 12 months and are allowed another 12 months to demonstrate that they are no longer failing. The post-inspection process is monitored by HMI.

By June 1995, 51 schools had been identified as failing since the start of OFSTED inspections in September 1993. These consisted of 28 primary schools, 19 secondary schools and four special schools. One school had improved sufficiently to be removed from the list. A number of others were considered to be making good progress. Two schools were to close and a further two had been proposed for closure. Up till that time the DFE had not found it necessary to instal an 'education association' in any of the schools although over the summer of 1995 it began to take steps to do so in one case.

A somewhat larger number of schools however (perhaps 5–10 per cent of all schools), while not technically failing, are considered to have serious weaknesses. These borderline cases are monitored by HMI. If they are found to have made insufficient progress they may be declared failing and thus become subject to special measures.

Not surprisingly, given the low incidence in absolute terms of failing schools, we had only one institution (Murbank Primary) in this category in our main sample of schools, although a couple were perhaps of borderline status. We therefore supplemented our evidence by contacting a further two schools. We consider below some of the issues arising from these two schools in the belief that they may also be relevant to other cases.

Reactions to failing: Coverley Primary School

Coverley is a smallish urban primary school which draws on a catchment area of privately owned and rented accommodation. The main criticisms made by the inspectors referred to: substantial underachievement in Key Stages 1 and 2; shortcomings in important aspects of pupils' learning; inconsistencies between classes and within subjects; poor planning and underdeveloped financial management and control.

We interviewed the headteacher on two occasions: first, a month after the end of the inspection and before the report had appeared; and second, three months later, after the report had appeared and the school had produced a draft action plan.

Unfortunate timing?

The headteacher felt that the inspection had occurred at a time when the school was under great difficulties with the deputy and school secretary both on long term absence due to sickness. The financial management of the school, for example, was largely entrusted to these two staff. The headteacher, anticipating retirement some time previously, had decided that it was better that training in financial management was concentrated on the deputy and secretary. With these two members of staff absent, the headteacher was struggling to maintain the financial system. This had additional consequences. First, the headteacher felt unable to devote enough time to staff in the lead-up to the inspection. Second, the need to cover the class of the absent deputy caused further difficulties:

> We had this teacher who came in part-time, mostly to do special needs work . . . with the deputy being off she very bravely took on the class teaching job. So we lost the person who had been doing special needs to the class teaching situation and that meant that we had to cover special needs so we had to bring in somebody new.

Special needs was one of the areas subsequently criticized in the report.

Given the circumstances the headteacher could have deferred the inspection but had decided not to do so for essentially altruistic reasons:

> Right at the beginning of the inspection the registered inspector said, 'Why did you go ahead with it if you had the opportunity to defer it?'. . . Obviously we should have done because it wasn't really going to give a true reflection of what we were all about . . . The reason really for not deferring was because of the staff. They didn't want it hanging over them for another couple of terms. Also I didn't want my successor to have to face an inspection as soon as they came in, within a term or two of taking over the reins as it were.

The headteacher was convinced that the 'snapshot' of the financial arrangements had been atypical:

> If you had asked me, shall we say, back in September how the results of the inspection would have gone, I'd have said they'd be sound with the financing and administration, the control of them. But when the time came, November to January, we were really struggling.

The inspection report did include a reference to the difficulties caused by the 'absence of staff with major roles in financial management and the lack of expertise of other staff in financial matters'. The headteacher, however, commented that this reference had only been included as result of the insistence of the chair of governors.

Shock at the claim of underachievement

Assessing the achievement of pupils is, perhaps, the most difficult of all the tasks which inspectors face. The Handbook requires that two forms of assessment be made wherever possible for each lesson inspected. The first is concerned with how achievements compare with national results and expectations, that is age-referenced achievements. The assumption here is that the level of achievement of the majority of pupils in a class can be identified and accurately assessed (at least in terms of a rating on a five-point scale) against some notion of a national norm. In most cases this requires the inspector to be able to relate specific achievements observed in particular lessons to broader National Curriculum levels. This is difficult enough, although for Coverley the inspectors assessed achievements as being generally appropriate for pupils' ages.

It was in the second form of assessment, where achievements were judged in relation to pupils' abilities, that the inspectors' were critical. In the absence of standardized test scores, pupils' abilities could only be inferred by inspectors from their observations and talks with pupils. Inspectors judged that achievements were not as high as their assessment of pupils' abilities would have suggested. In other words, the pupils were underachieving.

It was undoubtedly the inspectors' revelations of widespread underachievement that the headteacher and staff felt most hard to accept. The headteacher found it difficult to square comments in the report about children being well-motivated and hardworking with the claim that they were nevertheless under-achieving. It was also felt that pupils' subsequent careers at secondary school were generally in line with Coverley's expectations of their potential: 'Right from the beginning we've followed our children to see if they realized the potential we had in mind for them. Now with a few exceptions they've done that ... On the whole they've always fulfilled what our expectations were.' Moreover, the main secondary school to which pupils transferred was cited as saying that Coverley pupils were the best that it received.

The headteacher thought that the inspectors had based their judgements on an incorrect assessment of the proportion of able pupils in the school as a whole. In other words, the inspectors had overestimated what the bulk of pupils might be expected to achieve. The headteacher agreed that the general ability level of the intake to the school had improved in recent years and that this was particularly marked in the reception class. Indeed, the inspectors' judgement was that reception pupils had achieved standards 'in line with, or above, the national expectations for their age and satisfactory for their abilities'. The headteacher's view was that the proportion of able pupils in the other classes was not so high since intakes could, and did, vary over the years. It was claimed that across the school as a whole the ability range conformed to a normal curve of distribution. It has to be said, however, that since the school had not used any standardized testing in recent years, the headteacher's judgement could not be substantiated by reference to any 'objective' measures.

When asked whether the judgements made about underachievement had been challenged, the headteacher commented: 'Yes, you do feel like challenging it. But, I don't know, it's very difficult, very difficult to get satisfactory proof ... You just felt in many ways obliged to accept or to listen rather than to fight about it, you know.'

Where the headteacher had raised a question about this issue the inspectors tended to refer to the good quality of comment from individual pupils. The implication was that some pupils were 'bright' but that the learning they experienced was insufficiently challenging. The headteacher agreed with the former assessment but disagreed with the latter.

Turning round a failing school: the Burnden case

Burnden is a special school catering for a small number of secondary age boys with emotional and behavioural difficulties. It provides day and residential accommodation for the Loamshire LEA. The inspection report was not only highly critical of the quality, standards and efficiency of the general education provided but also of a number of more specific responsibilities pertaining to this kind of special school.

The school had been the subject of an LEA inspection around 15 months prior to the OFSTED inspection and some dozen key issues had been identified that needed addressing. Most of these were to be found, along with others, in the later OFSTED report.

The headteacher of the school had been absent on the last day of the OFSTED inspection due to sickness and had subsequently retired. The LEA had therefore acted quickly to second a senior member of its behaviour support service to the role of acting headteacher. The secondment lasted four terms and by the end of that period the school had been judged by HMI no longer to be failing and therefore no longer subject to special measures.

Our interview took place a couple of months after the end of the secondment when the acting headteacher had returned to the LEA. By this time a further acting headteacher had taken on the school pending a permanent appointment being made.

Initial response to the report

The report attracted substantial press coverage and initially there was a 'complete collapse of morale amongst the staff and the students'. About half of the staff felt the school had been hard done by and that the report was overly harsh and critical. Student behaviour deteriorated during the first term after the inspection. Parents, however, were generally supportive although only a small number turned up at meetings to discuss the report and, later, the action plan. No parents sought to withdraw their children.

The governors 'were fairly taken aback by the whole thing . . . and had not realised the position that the school was in'. The chair of governors resigned and a senior county councillor was appointed to the post. The task facing those taking on responsibility for the school was therefore a very challenging one. Reflecting on the experience the acting head[2] commented: 'I'd have to say for me personally it was the most stressful experience of my life. There's no question about that.'

With the appointment of the acting head and with the close support of the LEA a series of immediate changes were instituted pending the completion of a comprehensive action plan. The action plan was a 50-page A4 document. Each of the nine key issues identified in the inspection report was analysed into a series of separate tasks. For example, the key issue on the National Curriculum was translated into specific tasks for each of the nine main curriculum areas. In all, the nine key issues were analysed into 115 separate tasks. Each task was defined in terms of timescale for completion, resources needed, personnel responsible, and monitoring arrangements. In addition, 17 other aspects, not specifically included in the key issues, were identified as requiring action. These were not specified in such detail as the others.

Monitoring the action plan

HMI made three monitoring visits before agreeing to remove Burnden from the list of failing schools. The first was seven months after the publication of the report. Two HMI were involved – one who had led the OFSTED inspection and another who had not been involved the first time. The visit took place over two days and included observation of 14 lessons. A short report in the form of a letter indicated that the school was now much more effectively managed and that good progress had been made on several fronts.

The second visit took place four months later and again involved the two HMIs over two days and included observation of 13 lessons. The resulting 'letter' report showed that good progress had been made on implementing the majority of key issues. Some additional issues, not included in the original report, were also identified. These were generally minor ones concerned with the style of meals and residential facilities. One issue which had been the inspectors' concern all along was that the school should determine its own admissions policy and *raison d'etre*. The LEA did not think that this was realistic and was not prepared to budge on the matter and in the end OFSTED was prepared to let it go by.

The third visit took place over two full days, four months later and 17 months after the original inspection. A third HMI joined the team – the senior HMI for SEN – to moderate the findings of the other two. Twenty-three lessons were observed and discussions were held with the acting head, the chair of governors, and teaching staff. A full report was issued which found that all of the key issues from the previous inspection report had 'been tackled and most of the tasks set out in the action plan completed'; in brief, the school was 'no longer failing to give its pupils an acceptable standard of education'.

How was it done?

The acting head, reflecting on the experience, was very concerned to stress that it was very much the result of 'a concerted effort'. During the first 40 days, in which the action plan had to be completed, the acting head had initially worked closely with the local SEN inspector. The LEA had made an injection of funds amounting to £5000 to resource improvements to the curriculum. Two school closure days and a full weekend were given over to staff training. All subject inspectors came in on one of the closure days to work with staff on schemes of work, lesson planning and resources. The acting head paid generous tribute to the LEA: 'The LEA was incredibly supportive. And I have to say if I was a grant maintained school[3] without access to [such] resources I think we would have been in trouble. The resources of the authority were tremendously valuable at that time, and subsequently.' The regular monitoring visits and reports from HMI were also influential in ensuring that 'no "t" was left uncrossed'.

The acting head emphasized the importance of the action plan in giving the necessary sense of direction: 'What you have to have is a clear objective view of where it is you are going. If you haven't got that then I think it is too easy in a special school to get mired down in the day-to-day detail. Got to have some objectivity and I think the action plan gives you that.'

A key factor in improving teaching and learning standards was the introduction of 'individual education plans' (IEPs) for pupils. The monitoring (HM) inspectors had commended the use of IEPs and the move away from straightforward classroom teaching which they represented, towards a system based on each individual's academic and social needs.

The involvement of the headteacher in working with the staff was seen as essential:

> There was a lot of working with staff individually . . . We set up things like staff support groups and I had to have an open door policy of people always being able to come and talk about the difficulties they had and I tried never to be 'never mind that' but to be more lateral thinking than that and try to resolve problems.

The approach was summed up as

> really a mixture of being very clear about what it is you're doing and very clear about what you're going to be relentless and inexorable about and not ever back down from. And also [being clear about] those things where you will adopt a much more 'softly softly' approach and negotiate and deal with at the most constructive level you can.

The quality of staff was important:

> Well fundamentally I'd have to say it was a good staff. There were some very good people in the senior management team who . . . only needed to be managed in the sense of being delegated tasks. Once they were delegated they really ran with the ball and did some first class things, things like the IEPs that the deputy head and senior teacher did virtually on their own.

When asked whether the changes had actually become embedded in the school and would therefore be long-lasting the acting head was cautious. Momentum had to be maintained on the individual learning (IEP) front.

> I think that what's critical is that they see the need for working in that way. What they then find difficult is exactly how you do it. I mean that, on a day to day basis, if I'm planning my lesson and I've got six children in here all of whom present their own difficulties have I got then to prepare six different pieces of work? And how on earth do I find time to do that, and how do I reconcile it with National Curriculum requirements? And that is difficult . . . we're not just talking about differentiation of material but also presentation and behaviour management.

Another potential difficulty lay ahead, due to Loamshire's decision to reorganize its county-wide provision for SEN. As part of the reorganization plan, Burnden was about to change its remit in order to cater for pupils with *extremely* challenging behaviour. As a result, there would inevitably be some staff changes in creating what would effectively be a new school. This provides a salutary reminder that institutions are not necessarily enduring entities and that plans derived for a specific situation may have to be rethought for a different one in the future.

The inspection process and the 'failing' school

Failing schools point up particularly clearly the essential features of the inspection process. For example, the emotional consequences experienced by those undergoing inspection tend to be much more severe in schools deemed to be failing. This applies not only to school staff who frequently refer to their emotional state as one of 'trauma' and 'shock' but also, in some cases, to the inspectors; according to the headteacher of Coverley Primary, 'The registered inspector left in quite a distressed state . . . more distressed than I was. I suppose really because of knowing the detrimental effect it would have on us.'

Validity of judgements

Inspectors' judgements in such cases are also likely to be more fiercely contested than normally as headteachers and staff anticipate the all too likely possibility of being pilloried in the press. Newspaper headlines such as 'School for Dunces' accompanied the disclosures about Burnden School. Thus the importance that judgements are valid is nowhere more urgently underlined than in the extreme case of the failing school.

Of all the categories of judgement that the Handbook sets out, those concerned with 'standards of achievement', 'quality of learning', and 'quality of teaching' are crucial and at the heart of the inspection process. The assumption is that these three aspects can be sufficiently clearly distinguished for discrete judgements to be made on each. We are not so sure. Even if a sharp demarcation can be made conceptually between achievement and learning the task of reliably assessing the former in the relatively short period of time spent in a specific classroom composed of pupils of varying capabilities is formidable enough. The further claim to discern underachievement elevates the task to a still more challenging level of discrimination.

It must be remembered that the claim of underachievement, as in the Coverley inspection, is based on the aggregation of an unspecified number of inspector judgements related to individual subject areas. The reader of an inspection report can have no knowledge of the processes which led the inspectors to their judgements. The fact that there is usually a close similarity between descriptions of subjects expressed separately in 'achievement' and 'quality of learning' terms is no guarantee of the validity of either. Indeed we wonder whether inspectors tend first to make a judgement on the quality of learning and then *infer* from that the level of achievement attained.

We have the impression from reading the inspection report of Coverley that underachievement was the precipitating factor which moved the school decisively into the 'failing' category. Given the lack of reliable assessments of pupils' abilities available in the school, inspectors inevitably had to use their own judgements based on observation and the quality of pupils' comments. Whether or not those judgements were secure we cannot of course say. What we can say, however, is that inspection rests ultimately on a poorly understood notion of judgement. This is its Achilles' heel.

External support

As we have already observed, even if one accepts the validity of inspection findings they alone do not ensure that improvement follows. Failing schools represent the extreme case where the scale of improvement required is greatest. The case of Murbank Primary indicated the importance of external support. That was further underlined for Burnden School and extended in the recognition that support should be sustained over a substantial period of time.

Turning round a failing school is a major improvement project and is all too likely to require financial and other resourcing. The action plan for Coverley required an estimated additional expenditure of £11,000.

Action plans

The experience of Burnden indicates the importance played by a well-thought-out action plan. When we started our study we found that action plans, where they existed, were relatively primitive. In our later inspections it was clear that schools had gained considerable experience of their construction and that plans were more detailed in conception. This has undoubtedly been the result of OFSTED's own increasing sophistication in this area. Early guidance was relatively limited but by the summer of 1995 OFSTED's collective experience had been brought together into a compendium of good practice (OFSTED 1995d).[4]

Several aspects of action planning are particularly emphasized in this document. For example, it is stressed that action plans should not be confined to the key issues but should also take account of judgements made throughout the report. This wider consideration of judgements was apparent in the Burnden action plan. RgIs have also been reminded that key issues need to be clear, precise and manageable, and set in priority order. A major concern noted by OFSTED is that few plans include details of how implementation will be monitored and evaluated. The general format of plans has tended to follow that of school development plans by identifying tasks, responsible personnel, time-lines, resources and success criteria.

The Burnden action plan provides an exemplary model of this kind of approach to rational planning. A potential problem, however, is that a plan can become overly complex and difficult to comprehend and oversee. This may lead to difficulty of ownership by the staff as a whole. Related to this is the central assumption that each key issue should be tackled separately and independently of the others. We would suggest that a more likely approach would be to consider the key issues as a whole, identify possible interrelationships between them and then pose the question 'How may two or more of these issues be tackled in a single strategy?' More generally, the key issues need to be woven into a comprehensive strategy which embodies a vision capable of capturing the enthusiasm of staff. Our general assessment of the action plans we have seen is that they are worthy but dull.

The central question, of course, remains whether or not the implementation of an action plan leads to improved standards and achievements. This is recognized in OFSTED's exhortation that: 'In drawing up and revising their plans, schools should say how any proposed actions will raise the levels of pupils' achievements, the quality of education provided and the efficiency and effectiveness of the school' (OFSTED 1995d: 5). However, demonstrating that such fundamental changes do occur in practice is likely to be an enduring challenge.

9 SOME THEORETICAL
PERSPECTIVES ON
INSPECTION

> We fuzzies would like to substitute the idea of 'unforced
> agreement' for that of 'objectivity'.
>
> (Rorty 1991)

Inspection is one of those practices that *seems* to be self-evidently transparent – describable in terms of the apparently straightforward things that inspectors do. Anyone nowadays who asked the question 'What is inspection?' might be offered, as an answer, a copy of the Handbook to read. But practices are more complex than mere descriptions of what is (or should be) done. They are set within traditions and have origins and histories.

Some of the debates to which we refer in this chapter will be familiar to readers. Is inspection a rather naive form of 'positivism', for example, or does it attempt to draw to any significant extent on the assumptions and procedures underlying more interpretive approaches? What kinds of 'truth' claims can it make? How far are inspectors aware that they create an account of schools' performance that may not be shared? And is inspection recognizable as a form of educational evaluation? How important have recent attempts to extend auditing approaches and other forms of managerial control actually been and in what sense can inspection be said to be a form of auditing? How far is inspection merely a more subtle and sophisticated form of control over those responsible for providing education? When inspectors say that they have reached a consensus, what kind of consensus do they mean? And does it have a recognizable and defensible 'methodology' or is it simply, as some suspect, a rag-bag of 'methods'?

Those who practise inspection are often wedded to the view that it is 'common sense'. Consequently attempts to locate it within the Frameworks of social theorists have not, to our knowledge, been previously attempted. In this chapter we begin to explore the practice of inspection by looking at it from four different theoretical perspectives. First, as a form of educational evaluation and then as a form of auditing. We then go on to consider its influence as a 'disciplinary power' and finally reflect on its status as a form of social action.

Inspection as evaluation

In recent years inspection has increasingly been regarded as a form of evaluation (Wilcox 1989). Moreover, since the 1970s government policy has progressively settled on inspection as the dominant approach to the evaluation of schools. In our case studies we were able to assess the extent to which teachers and inspectors agreed with this development. We did so by asking whether they saw any feasible alternative to providing the kind of school account which inspection provides. One such alternative, widely canvassed during the 1970s, would have been self-evaluation.

Inspection contrasted with self-evaluation

We found little advocacy, in practice, for the alternative of self-evaluation amongst either group. The teachers interviewed at Ecclesley Secondary, for example, summarized many of the objections to self-evaluation raised in the other schools. Their remarks help, at the same time, to underline what they saw as the strengths of the inspection approach.

> In spite of the fact that we were aware of most of the issues [raised by the inspection] and working on them, self-assessment is incestuous and there is a need for an outside view.
>
> (Headteacher)

> In-house reports put great pressure on staff. No matter how neutral you are, there will still be bias.
>
> (Deputy headteacher)

> External review is objective and any other way would be too subjective.
>
> (Head of department (1))

> Self-evaluation takes a lot of time and there is a tendency to play down negative aspects in judging colleagues.
>
> (Head of department (2))

> There would always be problems with internal reviews which would damage relationships between colleagues.
>
> (Head of department (3))

It was also recognized that self-evaluation was 'unlikely to have the same breadth of focus' as inspection and that, therefore, a series of self-evaluations would need to be carried out over perhaps several years to achieve comparable comprehensiveness.

Occasionally self-evaluation was seen as a possibility, provided certain conditions were met. 'It can be done by people within school if the school has a highly developed school development planning process and information gathering procedures and opportunities for debate,' said one head of department at Potterton Secondary. 'It could be honest and open, reflecting what goes on, particularly if the report doesn't go outside the school.'

Self-evaluation with 'external moderation' was suggested as a possible alternative by a few inspectors and teachers. Such an approach was provided in the Sedley LEA. For example, Fenby Junior underwent a self-evaluation which was externally validated by the school inspector. The topic for evaluation was language – with reading as a special focus. The process took place over two days and was carried out by the school's language coordinator, the school inspector and the headteacher. The teachers tended to be in favour of this approach, emphasizing the teacher involvement associated with it and the value of having the impartiality of the inspector to provide the balance. The headteacher was also supportive of the approach, contrasting it with inspection '[which] is done to you whereas [self-]evaluation is done with you'.

The deputy saw it more as 'inspection with a friendly face' and thought that the alternative of an inspection would have given a similar although 'tougher' picture. The language coordinator, however, had several reservations:

> I would have been happier having two external people. This model felt much safer and lulled one into a false security. I felt this was an inspection – inspection on the cheap. I don't feel in control of the report. I do all the collection and . . . [name of inspector] says what to include. It is quite prescriptive and might as well be an inspection.

This particular self-evaluation had some of the features of 'joint inspection'. This was an approach mentioned on a couple of occasions elsewhere. For example, Forestshire inspectors had experimented in the past with joint inspections (that is with one or more teachers joining an inspection team)[1] until the practice had been discouraged by the influential chairman of their education committee.

In contrast to self-evaluation, inspection was generally accepted ('no real alternative') or at the very least regarded as a 'necessary evil'. This was the case generally with headteachers and their staff no less than with inspectors. Where the OFSTED Framework had been used it was generally commended. Some inspectors and teachers, however, considered that the LEA's former approach, although not so comprehensive, was preferable in being more developmental in nature. Different perspectives and priorities, they felt, could be more easily acknowledged.

The issue of objectivity

A frequently stressed advantage of inspection was its assumed greater 'objectivity' compared to the 'subjectivity' to which self-evaluation was considered prone. Related metaphors such as the need for 'external yardsticks' and 'extra pairs of eyes' abounded in interviewees' comments.

At least three distinct interpretations seem to lie behind the notion of objectivity. The first reflects the belief that inspectors are free from bias because they have no 'self-interest' in the schools they inspect and can therefore examine them impartially. This led some teachers to question the desirability of inspectors and schools having prior knowledge of each other. This, of course, is likely to be the case if a school is examined by inspectors drawn from its own LEA – a situation which is still possible under OFSTED arrangements, although with some safeguards against those with too close a relationship to the school.

A second interpretation of objectivity is the belief that the reality of a school can be described in terms of unambiguous 'facts': 'If a genuine objective picture, one based on *facts* is needed then, yes, a formal inspection is important'(Inspector, Potterton Secondary). However, this assumption was forcibly questioned by the headteacher of Alderman King Secondary: 'Schools are different things to different people – what it is like for one child is not the same for another. It will also not be the same for different teachers. I worry about the assumption that you can give authoritative accounts of schools . . . should we even attempt it at all?'

The third interpretation embodies what has been called 'procedural objectivity' defined as 'the development and use of a method that eliminates, or aspires to eliminate, the scope for personal judgement in the description and appraisal of a state of affairs' (Eisner 1991: 44). The achievement of procedural objectivity is the implicit assumption underlying the structure of the Framework and the Handbook and is particularly apparent in the attempt to specify explicit criteria for judgement.

Attitudes to inspection

This general sense of the inevitability and acceptability of inspection is at first glance somewhat surprising. Studies of LEA inspectorates and advisory services carried out in the mid-1970s and 1980s (Bolam *et al*. 1978; Stillman 1989; Stillman and Grant 1989) revealed little commitment to the regular and systematic evaluation or inspection of schools. Indeed some LEA inspectors of the period viewed the notion of engaging with schools in this manner as an inappropriate, almost improper, exercise of their position.

The consequences of the 1988 and 1992 Acts eventually had the effect of getting inspectors more involved in inspection. While this may have been simple compliance for some, for others the 'conversion' was undoubtedly more sincere: 'I am more effective as a change agent as a result of inspecting. Headteachers listen more to what I say now. Inspection provides a platform to move forward from' (Inspector, Tennyson Road Secondary).

In the past, teachers have also generally been hostile to the notion of inspection. They, too, have had to come to terms with the fact of inspection as a regular feature of their professional lives. Moreover, the way in which the process of inspection is understood both by inspectors and teachers is consistent with the government's overall approach to the role of evaluation in the public services.

Government's pursuit of objective evaluation

Henkel argues that the 1980s saw government giving a higher profile to a view of evaluation based on a positivist epistemology which assumed that 'complexities of provision can be broken down into definitively assessed or measurable indicators of performance' (Henkel 1991: 179–80). She suggests that this was all of a piece with the 'increasingly dominant trend ... to perceive the manager as superseding the professional as the force required to continue the successful rationalization of 20th-century society ... [where] the problems of complexity would be solved by quantitative technology and management skills' (Henkel 1991: 179–80).

Such shifts in practice ran counter to the shifts in evaluation theory 'that rejected concepts such as objectivity, saw evaluation as inevitably partisan, making choices as to which stakeholders they should regard as primary, and engaged in argument and negotiation ... rather than authoritative judgement' (Henkel 1991: 182).

The government's belief in value-free, objective evaluation was developed further in the Citizen's Charter (Cabinet Office 1991) where key reforms were proposed for the inspectorates covering the police, prisons, social services and schools. Inspectorates were defined as being 'concerned with value for money and standards of output and performance ... [and] to check the professional services that the public receives are delivered in the most effective way possible and genuinely meet the needs of those whom they serve' (Cabinet Office 1991: 40). It was claimed that the independence and objectivity of inspectorates could be at risk if they were 'captured by fashionable theories'. To counteract this tendency the Charter proposed that lay members be appointed to inspectorates so that the views of professional inspectors 'will be balanced by the *sound common-sense of the public*' (our emphasis, Cabinet Office 1991: 40).

In the case of schools, the Charter promised a review of HMI and changes which would result in 'independent judgement about schools, teaching and learning based on objective inspection and analysis of performance measures' (Cabinet Office 1991: 41). These commitments were subsequently included in the Parent's Charter (DES 1991a) and led eventually, as we have seen, to the 1992 Act and the setting up of OFSTED.

Thus the political rhetoric surrounding the emergence of OFSTED and the new inspection arrangements, subsequently enshrined in successive versions of the Framework and Handbook, reflected essentially positivist assumptions. Standards and measures of performance are regarded as relatively unproblematic educational 'facts' about schools that are to be identified by independent inspectors using objective methods and criteria.

Henkel disagrees. Drawing on the evidence of her study of four inspectorial public agencies (although educational inspectors were not included) and the well-established debates in the social sciences, she argues that *objective* evaluation is a myth. In her view: 'Evaluators bring with them values derived from occupational and disciplinary traditions, which may in turn be congruent with, or hostile to, the dominant political ideology' (Henkel 1991: 236).

It is quite clear that at the beginning of the 1990s HMI's tradition of inspection was viewed with suspicion by many Conservative politicians. That tradition, which was also reflected in the 'inspecting' LEAs of the time, was essentially 'about peer judgement by professionals reviewing the work of their fellow professionals . . . [and fitted], therefore, most neatly into the professional model of accountability' (Day and Klein 1987: 174–5). Such an approach ran counter to the government's distrust of professionals and its penchant for mana-gerial forms of accountability. As Jones and Moore (1995) have argued, attempts to secure this shift were part of a broader 'cultural change' agenda. The irony, however, was that when the Framework was constructed it was apparent that the HMI approach had been essentially retained. What resulted was less a radical recasting of the inspection process and more a modification of the traditional model incorporating the managerialist emphasis in the 1992 Act on performance, standards and efficiency.

Inspection, even in its current OFSTED form, does not fit neatly into the usual models of evaluation. It has some of the characteristics of positivist styles of evaluation – use of quantitative methods, the quantification of data, explicit criteria and the like. On the other hand, it also draws on some of the practices and assumptions which reflect the 'interpretive' and 'naturalistic' traditions of evaluation whilst not necessarily acknowledging that this is the case (see Wilcox 1992).

Inspection as auditing

In recent years the growth of audits across a range of public services has run alongside the growth of interest shown by government in inspection. The Citizen's Charter, for example, extolled not only the virtues of inspection but also those of audit:

> All public services should have efficient independent arrangements for audit. As in private businesses, this is essential if they are to be managed well. There is a further powerful stimulus to improvement when those outside a service are able to compare the performance of one body with that of others on a clear and consistent basis. Good external audit and inspection expose weaknesses. They confirm the reliability of good internal systems. They help to spread good practice, value for money and raise the quality of service.
>
> (Cabinet Office 1991: 38)

It is not only financial audits that are implied here but also the use of other quantitative data concerned with efficiency, quality and performance. 'League tables' of examination results, introduced by the Charter, represent perhaps the most familiar example of educational auditing.

The concepts of auditing are also incorporated into the inspection process itself. A key section in OFSTED reports on 'efficiency of the school' requires inspectors to report on such matters as: financial planning and control procedures; the efficiency and effectiveness of resource deployment; cost effectiveness and value for money. In examining financial and other resource documentation inspectors carry out tasks not dissimilar to those of auditors. Indeed inspection as a whole is reminiscent of an auditing process, with the Handbook and its detailed prescriptions representing the auditor's manual.

According to Power (1994) there has been a veritable 'audit explosion', not only in this country but throughout the developed world. Power argues that the need for audits arises from a radical reinvention of government in recent years. This has been informed by two opposing tendencies: devolution and decentralization of services on the one hand; and their control from the centre on the other. Such tendencies can be related to broader understandings of 'post-Fordist' developments in modern societies. Audits appear to be able to reconcile these tendencies better than the alternatives. The appeal of the audit idea is that it evokes a a cluster of desirable values: 'independent validation, efficiency, rationality, visibility almost irrespective of the mechanics and, in the final analysis, the promise of control' (Power 1994: 17).

Aspects of audits: some parallels with inspection

There are three aspects of Power's analysis of audits which cast an interesting light on inspection as practised under OFSTED. First is the notion of audit as 'control of control': 'One of the paradoxes of the audit explosion is that it does not correspond to more surveillance and more direct inspection. Indeed, audits generally act indirectly upon systems of control rather than directly upon first order activities' (Power 1994: 19). Inspection would seem to be an exception to this rule since inspectors clearly do focus on the first order activities of teaching and learning for much of their time. However, considerable attention is also paid to the second order activities which are assumed to exert an effect on how teachers perform in the classroom – these include the procedures, processes and types of documentation associated with management and administrative systems.

Some critics of OFSTED, such as Hargreaves, argue that inspections should be less concerned with first order activities (quality control) and that their primary purpose should be to check that a school puts in place 'mechanisms for monitoring its practices and establish[ing] procedures for designing and implementing changes in the interest of improvement' (Hargreaves 1995: 124). This would bring inspection more in line with audit practice and move it closer to a quality assurance perspective. To switch the emphasis in this manner, however, would be to lose an essential feature of inspection – that of observing the practice of teaching and learning directly in real time – which distinguishes it from other traditions of 'knowing schools' (Wilson 1995).

The second aspect is the view that audits make 'transparent' the internal workings of organizations to those who have an interest in them. As a result audits are thought to shift power from professionals and experts to stakeholders and the public. Power (1994) maintains, however, that although the findings of audits may be transparent the auditing *process*, the mechanisms by which organizations are made visible, is seldom subjected to critical scrutiny.

The informal aspects of 'occupational cultures', the shared assumptions and the working practices, remain obscured.

Once again OFSTED inspections would seem the exception. Not only are the reports of inspection open to all but so also is the Handbook. The Handbook sets out the inspection process in detail for anyone to see. However, as already noted, exactly how the detailed prescriptions are incorporated into the practice of actual inspectors remains largely a private and hidden affair – except in a limited sense to HMI which monitors the inspection teams. It is also significant that, although the Framework and Handbook have been extensively revised, the basic model of inspection and the assumptions underlying it continue essentially unchanged.

The third point is related to the second. Auditing is traditionally thought of as a neutral technique which is useful for representing certain financial or economic 'facts'. This in turn derives from the way in which financial and management accounting, the primogenitors of auditing, are widely regarded. This view has been challenged by radical critics of accountancy (such as Power and Laughlin 1992) who argue that it actually *creates* the very 'facts' that it purports to represent: 'Audits do not passively monitor auditee performance but shape the standards of this performance in crucial ways, [as well as] public conceptions of the very problems for which it is the solution' (Power 1994: 8).

There is a tendency, therefore, for any system of auditing to be self-referential and possibly tautological – to model organizations for its own purposes and thus to influence significantly their first order operations and to deny any notion of critical reflexivity in regard to their own processes. This is apparent in the way in which the Handbook has been received in many schools where it is has generally been hailed as a very useful 'management tool'. We noted earlier that the school model which the Handbook presents is regarded as unproblematic – indeed common-sensical. It is, however, one model amongst many and incorporates the assumption that schools can be described in terms of unambiguous, discrete management and pedagogic 'facts'.

There is a danger that schools will increasingly conform to a universal model. The likely result will be a reduction in the diversity of school types – an outcome

Table 9.1 Styles of auditing

Style A	Style B
Quantitative*	Qualitative*
Single measure	Multiple measures*
External agencies*	Internal agencies
Long-distance methods	Local methods
Low trust*	High trust
Discipline*	Autonomy
Ex post control	Real-time control*
Private experts*	Public dialogue

* = our suggested characteristics of inspection
Source: Power 1994

which, as Hargreaves (1995) notes, runs counter to a central feature of the Conservative government's avowed educational policy.

Power identifies two extreme types of model of control and accountability (Styles A and B) which vary on a number of key dimensions as outlined in Table 9.1. He maintains that the audit explosion has involved an overwhelming priority for Style A. He is careful, however, to disclaim the dogmatic view that in the shift to Style A there have been no gains at all. His position is that the gains are 'likely to be most visible when used in conjunction with, rather than in opposition to, Style B'. This view could also be said to apply to inspection. For while the public presentation of inspection tends to reflect Style A its actual practice also incorporates significant features of Style B.

Inspection as a disciplinary power

The history of school inspection goes back to the early years of the last century. As it emerged in the practice of HMI its foci were threefold: the testing of pupils, the assessment of teachers, and enquiring into the 'state' of schools. As inspection evolved over time these three aspects were progressively differentiated and today represent the separate activities of pupil assessment, teacher appraisal and school evaluation. School inspection is essentially about the third of these. It is teaching, rather than the individual teacher, which is evaluated and learning generally, rather than that of specific pupils.

Inspection appeared not only at the beginning of the public system of education but at a time when large numbers of individuals were being brought under the control of various kinds of institutions – factories, schools, barracks and prisons. Michel Foucault (1977) argues that such institutions developed from the mid-18th century with the emergence of the modern conception of government and the state. The new institutions gave rise to procedures having common characteristics constituting what Foucault calls *disciplinary power.* Disciplinary power '[i]nstead of bending all its subjects into a single uniform mass, separates, analyses, differentiates [them and] carries its procedures of decomposition to the point of necessary and sufficient single units' (Foucault 1977: 170).

Unlike the disciplines of the past which operated through 'the majestic rituals of sovereignty or the great apparatuses of the state', disciplinary power, Foucault argues, consists of 'humble modalities' and 'minor procedures'. Its success 'derives ... from the use of simple instruments: hierarchical observation, normalising judgement, and their combination in a procedure which is specific to it – the examination' (Foucault 1977: 170).

The inmates of disciplinary institutions were maintained under constant surveillance and supervision through *hierarchical observation.* This was ensured through the very architecture of schools, prisons, hospitals and the like – the whole forming a 'spatial nesting of hierarchised surveillance'. The aim of the new architecture was to 'permit an internal, articulated and detailed control – to render visible those inside ... to transform individuals: to act on those it shelters, to provide a hold on their conduct, to carry the effects of power right to them, to make it possible to know them, to alter them' (Foucault 1977: 172).

Disciplinary systems identified and controlled whole areas of individual behaviour largely neglected by the penal system. Instead a 'micropenality' was fashioned, concerned with punishing non-observance or departure from norms associated with time and attendance, correct behaviour and attitudes and the correct carrying out of specific tasks. *Normalizing judgements* are the regular assessments made of individuals against sets of norms and standards. They ensured a pervasive form of social control within institutions.

The role of the examination

It is in the *examination* that hierarchical observation and normalizing judgements are uniquely combined. Examination 'is a normalising gaze, a surveillance that makes it possible to qualify, to classify and to punish' (Foucault 1977: 172). It is a technology which is widespread not only in education but also in medicine, psychiatry, and the clinical and social sciences generally.

Foucault identifies three characteristics of the examination. First it exercises a disciplinary power which, while invisible itself, makes compulsorily visible those who are subjected to it and at the same time 'holds them in a mechanism of objectification'. Second, the procedures of examination situated individuals in a network of documentation as part of a 'meticulous archive' which captured and fixed them. As a result the subject became a describable, analysable object. This, in turn, made possible the comparison of individuals and the determination of population distributions. Third, examination (and its documentary techniques) makes each individual a 'case':

> The case is no longer, as in casuistry or jurisprudence, a set of circumstances defining an act and capable of modifying the application of a rule; it is the individual as he may be described, judged, measured, compared with others, in his very individuality who has to be trained or corrected, classified, normalized, excluded, etc.
>
> (Foucault 1977: 191)

The examination provides 'the pinning down of each individual in his own particularity . . . [and] clearly indicates the appearance of a new modality of power in which each individual receives as his status his own individuality, and in which he is linked by his status to the features, the measurements, the gaps, the "marks" that characterise him and make him a "case" ' (Foucault 1977: 192).

Disciplinary power and management

Disciplinary power is apparent in much of present-day management; it is seen as a means to organizational efficiency and control. Participants in management cultures, however, rarely see things in these ways – they refer, instead, to such notions as 'empowerment'. In education, for example, Ball argues that appraisal has become a major mechanism in the reconstruction and disciplining of teachers as ethical subjects: 'It extends the logics of quality control and performance indicators into the pedagogical heart of teaching. It brings the tutelary gaze to bear, making the teacher calculable, describable, and comparable' (Ball 1990: 159).

Disciplinary power has also been extended from an exclusive focus on the individual to that of the school. Not only must teachers be reconstructed and disciplined but so also must the schools in which they function. Inspection is now seen as a major means in the improvement of schools – in some accounts, indeed, it is treated almost as if it were a form of 'empowerment'.

Hierarchical observation is built into the very structure of OFSTED. Inspection teams observe individual schools. Registered inspectors are expected to monitor the performance of their inspectors. RgIs and their teams are in turn monitored by HMI.

Inspection is the examination of a whole school resulting in a multiplicity of normalizing judgements made by applying criteria, rating scales and judgement-recording statements. The outcome is an account of the school cast in the various descriptors of institutional 'good' and 'evil' such as: strengths and weaknesses; success and failure; effectiveness and ineffectiveness; efficiency and inefficiency. Inspection creates a school as a case with its associated dossier or 'record of inspection evidence'. It effectively locates an individual school on a continuum of cases ranging from the 'excellent' and 'successful' to the 'failing'.

An inspection is disciplinary in two senses. It requires a school to undergo an exacting discipline which extends over a period considerably longer than that of the inspection week. Inspection may also lead to a school being 'disciplined'. Thus those who are associated with any weaknesses identified in an inspection always risk censure not only by those within the school community but also by those outside the school. Major shortcomings are exposed and expected to be remedied. In the extreme case of a 'failing' school there is not only the likelihood of public opprobrium but also an additional period of surveillance and the possibility of eventually being taken over by an 'educational association'.

Inspection as panopticon

The enduring metaphor which Foucault employs for the permanent visibility of subjects achieved through disciplinary power is Bentham's *panopticon*.[2] This was conceived of as a circular architectural structure composed of cells each containing an inmate. The cells were so arranged that they and their inmates could be kept under constant surveillance.

OFSTED could be seen as the new inspection *panopticon* which keeps some 24,000 school 'cells' and their teacher 'inmates' under surveillance. OFSTED's 'gaze' is focused on schools through the instrument of the Handbook. This has been described by one influential secondary headteacher as 'the best book on school management which has ever appeared from official sources. It is a well-polished mirror in which to reflect – and reflect upon – the performance and procedures of all areas of school life' (Matthews and Smith 1995: 25–6). Indeed there is some evidence that the Handbook is being used as a tool for school self-evaluation and a vehicle for staff and management development

(Matthews and Smith 1995; 26). As a result of the internalization of the disciplines of the Handbook in this way, the OFSTED 'gaze' is maintained between inspections – surveillance effectively becomes continuous.

This brief consideration of the relevance of Foucauldian concepts is important for two reasons. First, it reminds us that inspection has its own substantial history. Second, it forces us to confront the realization that the origins of inspection are to be found in the ' "ignoble" archives, where the modern play of coercion over bodies, gestures, and behaviour has its beginnings' (Foucault 1977: 191).

Inspection as a form of social action

The inspection of schools is clearly a complex social process consisting of innumerable interactions between inspectors, teachers and others. How might such a process be understood in terms of social action? We have found no sustained analysis of inspection from this kind of sociological perspective. We consider, however, that the views of the influential social theorist Jurgen Habermas are fruitful for illuminating its nature.[3] To justify this point we shall draw here on some concepts developed in *The Theory of Communicative Action* (Habermas 1984; 1987).

Strategic and communicative action

Habermas sees social action – human interaction – being coordinated through the medium of language. He draws a sharp distinction between two types of social action. In *strategic action* an actor is oriented to intervening in a social context according to the criteria of effectiveness or success:

> a *strategic* model [is] when there can enter into the agent's calculation of success the anticipation of decisions on the part of at least one additional goal-directed actor. This model is often interpreted in utilitarian terms; the actor is supposed to choose and calculate means and ends from the standpoint of maximizing utility.
>
> (Habermas 1984: 85)

In contrast, the concept of *communicative action* refers

> to the interaction of at least two subjects capable of speech and action who establish interpersonal relations ... The actors seek to reach an understanding about the action situation and their plans of action in order to coordinate their actions by way of agreement. The central concept of *interpretation* refers in the first instance to negotiating definitions of the situation which admit of consensus.
>
> (Habermas 1984: 86)

These distinctions are not merely analytic but fundamental in that any competent social actor can be expected to make them:

> I am in fact supposing that the actors themselves, in every phase of interaction, can know – however vaguely and intuitively – whether they are

adopting a strategic-objectivating attitude towards other participants or are oriented to consensus . . .'

(Habermas 1982; quoted in Roderick 1986: 109–110)

Validity claims and the 'ideal speech situation'

In order to understand the significance of communicative action it is necessary to know something of Habermas's view of language. Habermas holds that a speaker comes to an understanding with another person about something in the world by raising three distinct *validity claims*. In every utterance a speaker makes a *truth* claim relating to the *objective world*, a *rightness* claim relating to the *social world* of normatively regulated interpersonal relations, and a *truthfulness* or *sincerity* claim relating to the speaker's *subjective world*. Thus we can ask of any speaker 'Is what you say true?', 'Are you entitled to say that?', and 'Do you really mean it?'

These claims are universal features of linguistic communication – they are raised implicitly or explicitly in every speech act. In addition, each lays claim to universal validity for what it claims to be true, right or truthful. In other words, validity means validity for everyone capable of speech and action. 'With any utterance, then, a speaker lays claim to three dimensions of validity that *transcend* the particular context in which the utterance is made' (Hohengarten 1992: x).

The extent to which an utterance is valid is determined by examining the *reasons* that a speaker can give in support of what is said and the extent of their acceptability by others in the process of *argumentation* which is

> that type of speech in which participants thematize contested validity claims and attempt to vindicate them or criticize them through arguments. An *argument* contains reasons or grounds that are connected in a systematic way with the *validity claim* of a problematic expression. The 'strength' of an argument is measured in a given context by the soundness of the reasons; that can be seen in, among other things, whether or not an argument is able to convince the participants in a discourse, that is, to motivate them to accept the validity claim in question.
>
> (Habermas 1984: 18)

Even in situations where reasons are neither actually demanded nor given, the meaning of every speech act is tied to the potential of reasons that *could* be given in support of it. 'In this sense, every speech act points implicitly to the argumentative procedure of giving and evaluating reasons in support of validity claims' (Hohengarten 1992: x).

When speakers take part in argumentation they must suppose that certain conditions hold to ensure that agreements reached are based on reasons alone and not, for example, on power relations among speakers. These conditions define what Habermas calls the *ideal speech situation*. Although, in practice, argumentation may not often correspond to this ideal, it is more than a fiction for it plays an essential and formative role in communication. Habermas suggests the following 'rules' as constitutive of an ideal speech situation.

1   each subject is allowed to participate in discussion;
2a each is allowed to call into question any proposal;
2b each is allowed to introduce any proposal into the discussion;
2c each is allowed to express his attitudes, wishes, and needs;
3   no speaker ought to be hindered by compulsion – whether arising from inside the discussion or outside it – from making use of the rights secure under 1) and 2).

(White 1988: 56)

Inspection: strategic or communicative action?

The essential task of any inspection team is to reach agreement about the educational quality of a school. This is most easily accomplished, the Handbook suggests, through discussion involving all team members towards the end of the inspection. However, it is rather brief about the form such discussion(s) should take. Do we have here, then, an example of communicative action and an attempt to implement an idealized speech situation?

We have already noted in an earlier chapter some of the practical problems that can arise in such meetings. For example, not all inspectors may in fact be present during the final meeting held before the feedback of findings to senior school staff (rule 1 above). There is also the fact that the composition of an inspection team – registered inspector, inspectors and lay inspector – constitutes a status hierarchy and thus a *de facto* power hierarchy. This may result in effects which limit the extent to which true attitudes, feelings and needs are actually expressed (rule 3).

A major external 'compulsion' (rule 3) is that of time. Inspection is an extreme example of 'time-constrained evaluation' (Wilcox 1992). A vast amount of data has to be collected, analysed and interpreted in a very short period of time. At each stage of inspection time is perceived as a major constraint. The practice of holding the final team meeting on the penultimate day of the inspection, in order to meet the feedback requirements for the final day, may leave insufficient time to allow the achievement of true consensus.

In a survey of inspections of primary schools OFSTED monitors found that in many team meetings 'the quality of professional debate was impressive; issues were resolved and the full range of judgements . . . were corporately agreed on the basis of sound and wide-ranging evidence' (OFSTED 1995e: 7). There were, however, examples of 'judgements being accepted by the team without rigorous debate'.

Team meetings therefore may be regarded in *some cases* as approximating to communicative action and the ideal speech situation. The approximation is more remote in meetings involving inspectors and school staff. The fact that these are designated as 'feedback' sessions indicates that their purpose is to deliver judgements which have already been formed. Although inspectors are willing to correct 'errors of factual accuracy' no modification of the judgements themselves is usually entertained. Any attempt at reaching joint understanding and agreement in such meetings is therefore minimal – the situation is almost overwhelmingly one of strategic rather than communicative action.

The same is true for the interactions between individual inspectors and individual teachers. The inspector essentially adopts an objectivating attitude to the teacher. The expectation is that the inspector interprets the teacher's behaviour within the criteria and detailed prescriptions of the Handbook. These are non-negotiable, as are the judgements made. Although inspectors are encouraged to seek the perspective of teachers through scrutiny of lesson plans and discussion, the pressures of the hectic inspection timetable severely limit the possibilities. There is neither the time, nor indeed the obligation, to obtain an agreed synthesis of views. It is the inspector's view which remains privileged.

Inspection is, therefore, essentially an example of strategic action involving inspectors and teachers, although a somewhat aetiolated form of communicative action may be discerned in the engagement of inspectors with each other.

Inspection as a steering mechanism

Habermas is concerned not only with social action at the micro-level but also with providing a description of the modernization of society as a whole. We turn now to a brief summary of his views on the latter and to their relevance to inspection seen as a major government intervention.

Habermas interprets modern society in terms of the interaction between 'the lifeworld', 'systems', and 'steering media'. The *lifeworld* is the context within which communicative action occurs and the 'horizon' within which people refer to aspects of the objective, social and subjective worlds. It consists of 'more or less diffuse, always problematic, background convictions . . . [which] serve as a source of situation definitions that are presupposed as unproblematic . . . it also stores the interpretive work of preceding generations' (Habermas 1984: 70). In modern society the lifeworld undergoes a process of *rationalization* in which the three worlds are structurally differentiated into the three dimensions of culture, society and personality. The maintenance of these structural components is achieved through processes of 'cultural reproduction', 'social integration' and 'socialization' respectively.

Systems emerge from the lifeworld as functionally definable arenas of action. The principal ones are the economic and administrative systems and these are guided by lifeworld concerns and held together by the *steering media* of money and power. According to Habermas *colonization of the lifeworld* takes place when the steering media begin to penetrate the reproduction processes of the lifeworld. Thus the communicative infrastructure of the lifeworld, constituted by understanding-oriented action, is displaced by action coordinated by money and power requiring only an objectivating attitude and an orientation to success – in other words, by strategic action (White 1988: 110).

Although colonization may lead to enhanced material reproduction, above a certain threshold this will be outweighed by consequent effects on the processes of symbolic reproduction. The result will be the appearance of 'pathological' side-effects: loss of meaning, alienation, anomie, and withdrawal of legitimation. This is the case, Habermas believes, in advanced industrial societies.

Habermas's model has been refined by Broadbent *et al.* (1991) who recognize that societal steering media and systems are themselves made up of a wide range of institutions and organizations with their own micro lifeworlds, steering media and systems. This has enabled the model to be used as an evaluative device for assessing the effects of a range of government initiatives in the National Health Service. A similar exercise might be carried out for the Education Service.

Inspection as 'colonization'

The list that follows shows how the model might apply to OFSTED inspections. The crucial question to be asked is whether OFSTED inspections colonize the lifeworld of schools to the extent of producing pathological effects as Habermas might lead us to suspect.

OFSTED: a societal steering medium
Inspections: a steering mechanism
Schools: a societal system.

Broadbent and her colleagues suggest that the colonizing potential of steering media may be assessed by applying two 'rules of thumb' advanced by Habermas (1987: 364–73). The first is whether or not the steering media are of a 'regulative' or 'constitutive' character. The former is concerned with regulating some pre-existing, ongoing activity such as, for example, the rules for safe driving. The latter is where some form of activity is actually created (or constituted) such as the rules of chess. Regulative rules are claimed to be 'freedom-guaranteeing' while constitutive rules are 'freedom-reducing' and 'actually constitute systems behaviour distinct from accepted norms and guiding lifeworld intentions'.

The second rule of thumb is whether steering media are 'amenable to substantive justification' or only 'legitimised through procedure' (Habermas 1987: 365). 'Put simply, all steering media will be directed by official bodies . . . Where it is comprehensible to the "average individual" and, therefore, somehow reflects "informed common-sense" it will not need much defending' (Broadbent *et al.* 1991: 7).

The evidence from our own research indicates that for most schools OFSTED inspections are constitutive and freedom-reducing. This is because prior to the 1992 Act inspection had been, if at all, an occasional rather than a regular ongoing activity. Even in those LEAs which had well-established programmes pre-1992, the experiences (and consequences) of inspection were of a different order to those under OFSTED with its statutory basis and high political profile.

Where the second rule is concerned the situation is a little more complex. When the new inspection arrangements were first mooted they met with widespread opposition in schools and elsewhere. As the arrangements for the new inspections became clearer, and certainly in the early inspections, acceptance was more apparent. In particular, the initial reception of the Framework and Handbook by teachers was generally favourable. It seems that once the fact of regular inspection had been accepted there was considerable support for the

OFSTED approach, particularly amongst senior staff. Although the inspection Framework has been modified to make it more manageable, it is significant that the essential elements have remained intact and continue to be endorsed by many teachers.

Thus, although colonization does undoubtedly occur during an inspection and can engender some manifestations of collective and individual pathologies, these may not be long-lasting. After inspection the lifeworld of schools may revert to normal. However, it may be that inspection is simply the latest in a line of management-oriented initiatives from government that have *already* colonized the educational lifeworld and fundamentally changed its values towards those of a managerialist nature.

Conclusion

This examination of inspection through four separate pairs of 'conceptual spectacles' clearly points up its central problematic. This may be expressed succinctly in the question 'On what authority are the knowledge claims of inspection based?' The advocates of inspection rest its authority on notions of objectivity, contrasted with mere subjectivity and linked implicitly, if not explicitly, with a belief in the clear separation of facts and values. Ironically, the 'objectivity' rhetoric of inspection is at variance with much of its actual practice. Inspection tends to be regarded as a neutral technique, a mirror held up to the 'reality' of the school. Inspection, however, is itself a 'constituting' practice, creating the Framework within which schools are described.

The objectivity and the associated validity problematic cannot be resolved simply by increased attention to the details of methods and procedures. Objective truth is a *chimera*. Statements about schools are not like pictures which can be more or less like what they represent. We cannot break out of the linguistic domain which is the only place where the validity claims embodied in speech acts can be clarified. What we can achieve is agreement on how situations will be interpreted. Whilst reaching consensus cannot guarantee 'truth', it does represent a rational form of life. In other words inspection, if not an objective practice, can at least be a rational one, capable at the same time of some critical reflexivity about its own assumptions and procedures.

10 LOOKING TO THE FUTURE

> Study the past if you would divine the future.
>
> (Confucius)

In the first part of this chapter we summarize the main insights from our study and review of school inspection. These are expressed as a number of related general issues. In the second part we draw on some of the issues to suggest how inspection might develop in the future.

Inspection: general issues

Inspection is not simply a set of methods and procedures but a complex social practice which has developed over time

Having a history implies a sense of continuity with the past. The essential concerns of inspection have persisted since its earliest days – these include what we now refer to as 'accountability', 'standards' and 'quality' and 'value for money'. To be located in history means being influenced by the socio-political climate of the times. Consequently the fortunes of inspection have waxed and waned; during some periods its political profile has been high, at others imperceptible. Since the late 1980s inspection has been in the ascendancy and at the centre of educational politics.

History is also characterized by occasions of radical discontinuity with the past. The period 1990–2 marked the most recent such occasion in the long history of inspection. This was a time of mounting suspicion in some quarters about the independence of HMI, LEAs and educational 'providers' generally. It was also a time when the government's unbridled confidence in applying the virtues of the market to public services was arguably at its height. It was from this context that the system of OFSTED inspections emerged.

Government claims about the lack of systematic monitoring and evaluation of schools in LEAs in the immediate period post-ERA were unduly pessimistic

By 1990/1 the majority of LEAs were seriously addressing the government's newly-introduced policy of 'inspection in all its forms'. Up to 80 per cent of LEAs were conducting substantial exercises in at least some of their schools. In a small minority of LEAs inspections were being conducted with a frequency that was approaching the four-yearly cycle subsequently envisaged by OFSTED. Had the government so wished, existing approaches to inspection (which included some particularly innovative variants) could have been further encouraged. Some LEA approaches embraced strategies for dealing with issues which have emerged in criticisms of the OFSTED model such as the importance of post-inspection support.

Approaches to the monitoring and evaluation of schools in the pre-OFSTED period may be appropriately described in terms of the two factors 'coverage' and 'extent of teacher involvement'

OFSTED inspections constitute an inspection 'type' defined by a high level of coverage (being the most comprehensive of 'full' inspections) and a low level of teacher involvement in the inspection process. In contrast, self-evaluations correspond to high levels of teacher involvement. By the early 1990s 'full' or even 'part' self-evaluations were very rare occurrences. However, self-evaluation had survived, at least notionally, incorporated as a component of school development planning.

The extent and nature of teacher involvement varied considerably and was reflected in the titles used to describe inspection (e.g. 'consultative', 'negotiated', 'contract') and in the emphasis given by many chief inspectors to 'collaboration' and 'partnership' in their relationships with schools.

The period 1992–4 saw an increasing trend in LEAs towards accepting the notion of performance standards for schools

In the pre-OFSTED period LEAs tended to regard the raising of educational standards as being a consequence of their promotion of more general curriculum and INSET initiatives. Inspection was often included among the initiatives cited by chief inspectors, although it was not necessarily considered the most important. Where improvements were claimed these were invariably in terms of standards of *process* rather than of *performance* or *outcome*.

Towards the end of our fieldwork in 1994 an increased interest was being shown by chief inspectors in the development of quantitative standards of performance and 'value added' analyses. The influence of the government's promotion of 'league tables' and the introduction of OFSTED with its emphasis on quality and standards was clearly apparent.

Despite the 'surface' differences between the various approaches to inspection there is a broadly common underlying methodology

This common methodology consists of an invariant sequence of the various stages of inspection and a set of similar methods and procedures. At the heart of the process – its methodological core – is the view that judgements are made on the basis of a systematic review of evidence against specific criteria. This common methodology is incorporated in the OFSTED Handbook in its most explicit and developed form to date.

The OFSTED Handbook embodies not only a model of inspection but also an implicit model of the school

The school model is based essentially on the one implicit in HMI's pre-OFSTED approach to secondary school inspections suitably modified by the specific requirements of Section 9 of the 1992 Act. The model represents a culmination of the growing trend in recent years to regard schools essentially as management systems concerned with the delivery of specific standards of performance and quality.

The OFSTED system for the delivery of inspections represents a radical departure from former practice

The innovative features of OFSTED's approach lie in its delivery system including: extension of the traditional recruitment base of inspectors; speedier methods of reporting; high frequency of inspection (four-year cycle); and, most radical of all, the contract/tendering arrangements involving 'independent' inspection teams.

Criticisms of the Framework and Handbook have generally referred to the logistics of delivery rather than to the methodology of inspection or the model of the school

OFSTED has been assiduous in addressing criticisms of the Framework and Handbook by modifying the arrangements for inspection and revising both documents. The aim has been to reduce the burden of inspection demands on schools and to increase the manageability of the task for inspectors.

In comparison, criticisms of the underlying methodology have been relatively few and even fewer have been those directly concerned with the model of the school. Both of these aspects are considered as relatively unproblematic by the majority of inspectors and school staff. The apparent general acceptance of the Framework and Handbook is a noteworthy phenomenon given the almost universal hostility directed at the arrangements when first mooted in 1991.

The validity of individual inspections can never be definitively assured –
all are potentially prone to one or more validity threats

Critical comments on the methods of inspection, although not proportionately
great, tended to indicate that the credibility of inspection findings could be viti-
ated by uncertainties about sampling, the context in which judgements were
made, the application of evaluation criteria and the effective corroboration of
judgements (particularly as exercised through consensual agreement during
meetings of the inspection team). Such uncertainties are made more likely by
the combination of the sheer comprehensiveness of an OFSTED inspection and
the comparatively limited time in which it must be accomplished.

Threats to validity can be minimized although never completely eliminated.
Inspection, like other forms of educational evaluation, is never unassailable.
In the end, an inspection has persuasive power rather than definitive validity.
An inspection relies on the expectation that the inspectors are trusted to make
'expert' judgements.

Inspection as currently conceived provides an example of the 'work
intensification' hypothesis

Inspection has the effect of further intensifying teachers' work, particularly
those with management roles. Intensification is not confined simply to the
actual period of inspection but extends retrospectively in preparing for the
inspection and prospectively in responding to its findings. Under OFSTED
arrangements the work of inspectors has also been significantly intensified. In
both cases, intensification may lead to high stress levels.

Inspection by its very nature is prone to generate feelings of anxiety

The prospect (and often the actual experience) of inspection generates anxiety
in many teachers. This is probably inevitable since, from the individual
teacher's standpoint, inspection opens a window on the 'professional self'.
Possibly related to this is the frequent teacher complaint that inspection allows
insufficient time for the provision of adequate feedback.

Some inspectors may also experience anxiety arising from the fear that they
will fail to do what is expected of them by their colleagues. Both teachers and
inspectors feel, in their different ways, that their competence is on the line
during an inspection. For the majority of teachers, however, any anxiety is
likely to be short-lived and not seriously disabling.

Inspection as generally practised seems to produce only limited gains in
new knowledge and insights for the teachers involved

One of the most frequent comments that teachers made about inspection was
that there had been 'no great surprises'. However, as our interviews unfolded
it often became apparent that there had, in fact, been some surprises.
Nonetheless, senior staff in schools tended to feel that they could have written

the report themselves. Nothing remarkable was turned up it seemed *except* (and this was an important exception) where a school was 'at risk' and didn't know it.

Given its resource intensity we are led to wonder whether inspection should (or could) be a significant 'learning experience' and, if not, whether it is a cost effective way of generating predictable insights for teachers. However, teachers also frequently commented that inspection had served other useful purposes. These included providing a boost for teacher morale by public recognition of what the school had achieved, and clarifying and/or confirming priorities for future development.

In contrast, inspectors learnt a lot from inspection, even where they had little prior familiarity with the schools involved. In the past, such knowledge might have informed any subsequent development work which the inspectors undertook with a school after inspection. This is a less likely outcome now, however, given the constraints imposed by the 1992 Act.

The extent to which individual schools were able to implement the findings of inspection was very varied

The pattern of implementation of inspection recommendations or key issues for action was very patchy. Most schools claimed to have made a start but up to a year or so following inspection only about a quarter of recommendations had been subtantially implemented and nearly 40 per cent remained essentially unimplemented. Some six or so further months on there was some additional, albeit modest, improvement. For example, no school had fully implemented more than two thirds or so of its recommendations and the majority had implemented only half or less.

Implementation of individual recommendations varied according to the specific characteristics of the recommendation and the immediate context

The extent of implementation of a recommendation was influenced by its inherent 'complexity', the validity and importance ascribed to it by the senior management team in particular, and the quality of the implementation strategy adopted. The latter was in turn affected by the qualities and skills of the school's senior management team and teachers, the staffing and organizational structures, the availability of resources, any concurrent local/national initiatives, and any external support from the LEA or elsewhere. So-called 'failing' schools may have particular difficulties in several of these respects.

The literature of school improvement and educational change would suggest that expectations of substantial implementation of inspection findings within short time scales will, for many schools, be overly optimistic

The key issues for action arising from an OFSTED inspection and the action plan derived from them will generally constitute a substantial programme of school-wide change – particularly so in the case of the 'failing school'. None of the schools in our sample had reached the 'institutionalization' and 'outcome' phases of Fullan's model of educational change. If this model applies to the generality of inspections we would expect timescales well in excess of 18 months or so to be necessary for substantial changes to become embedded and discernible changes in teaching and pupils' learning to occur.

It remains to be seen whether the additional guidance to be given on the design of action plans and the provision of specifically targeted post-inspection funding from 1995/6[1] will lead to a reduction of the lengthy time-scales normally associated with major initiatives. In many cases schools will have to draw on skills and capacities which they possess in merely embryonic form or even not at all.

The issue of validity is logically prior to any consideration of whether the changes arising from inspection constitute improvement

It is assumed that the key issues for action represent a valid agenda for 'improvement'. This assumes that they appropriately reflect the main findings of the inspection, which in turn are a valid summary of the myriad of judgements made throughout the report. Validity threats can clearly occur at each of these stages.

Finally such judgements are premised on the validity of the methods adopted and the school model embodied in the inspection process. 'Improvement', in the final analysis, therefore implies changes which bring a school into ever closer congruence with the OFSTED model of the school.

OFSTED inspections embody a belief in management rationality

The essential characteristic of educational reform in recent years has been a radical shift away from a professional discourse to a managerial/bureaucratic one. Teachers and their work have been increasingly subjected to the dictates of a management rationality which treats concepts like 'efficiency' as neutral technical matters. Inspection represents the latest in a line of government initiatives based on such assumptions. In Habermasian terms this can be understood as strategic action colonizing the communicative structures of the teachers' lifeworld whereas, from a Foucauldian perspective, management is about the subjugation of bodies; it is essentially a 'disciplinary power'.

Management rationality may be a necessary condition for school improvement but not a sufficient one. School leaders who ignore aspects of 'collegiality' and 'shared decision-making' do so at their peril. Educational change is facilitated by visions as well as mandates.

Rethinking some assumptions and constructing a future

Shortly after Chief Inspector Woodhead took over leadership of OFSTED in 1994 he announced a major review of the ways in which the agency was setting about its tasks. A number of important changes and reforms resulted. In this concluding section we set our minds briefly to the same kind of agenda. Efforts to secure greater accountability need, we believe, to be conducted with a keener eye to their likely effects on improvement and vice versa.

Strategies for modifying the nature of accountability

So where would we start? First, with the frequency with which schools were exposed to 'full' inspections. By extending the cycle simply by a single year a considerable resource can potentially be released. OFSTED has committed itself to covering all the schools in the country within a four-year cycle. We are not sure why four years was chosen. It is not a figure which emerges from any of the literature on school effectiveness or school improvement with which we are familiar, except to the extent that it is a time-frame which is in the middle distance. A shorter gap might be too short to allow schools to demonstrate that they had really begun to improve. On the other hand, if inspection is to serve some kind of accountability function, then the gap between such inspections should not be too long – periods beyond seven years might be too infrequent. The only obvious virtue of the four-year gap seems to be a political one – if all the schools in the country are covered within this time-span, then the chances are all will have been inspected before the next General Election. Our preference would be for a five-year gap. If this policy were to be adopted, two out of every ten schools would be inspected per year.

Our second concern would be to make greater use of random sampling. For too long Chief Inspectors have been put in the invidious position of having to pretend that the best picture of the state of the nation's schooling is the one which is based on the largest numbers available. The extent to which such a picture might become 'biased' (a technical term) because of particular policy initiatives declared by successive Secretaries of State (to focus, for example, on grant-maintained or disadvantaged schools) has been ignored. A carefully-structured, randomly chosen national sample (or one which was constructed after the event to have the same characteristics) based on one school in ten would suffice; it would after all cover, in any single year, some 400 secondary schools and some 2000 primaries. Such an arrangement would free up a considerable inspection 'resource' and allow a little more flexibility to be exercised with respect to what precisely was inspected in the other schools. From the point of view of the schools it is doubtless the fact that they have been 'inspected' which matters, rather than the precise contribution they have made to the greater scheme of things.

The resources released by this decision to involve only one in ten schools in any one year in a national sampling exercise could be used first to identify schools in trouble and then to follow up and support them. Local 'intelligence' could be employed to assist in identifying where the remaining inspections should be concentrated. Up to 400 inspections of secondary schools could be deployed in this way. It is still something of an irony that halfway through the first cycle of inspections the question of whether most of the 'failing' schools in the country had been identified, or merely those that had turned up, remained unanswered. If the former, then the numbers revealed were encouragingly low; if the latter, then it seems extraordinary, given the depths to which some 'failing' schools appear to have sunk, to have waited up to another two years before taking appropriate action. Another small part of the resources could be used, as Burchill (1995) has suggested, to ensure that LEAs (or similar bodies) took a 'watching brief' in relation to schools' performances, using such monitoring data as were readily to hand on an annual basis.

At the time of writing the Framework and Handbook were undergoing considerable revision and some pruning. Of course, pruning was essential. The ring binders containing advice to inspectors had stretched well beyond 400 pages and were beginning to break under the strain as update followed update. To a large extent, however, the experience seems to have borne out our maxim that when two or more educators are gathered together and can't agree, they simply add things to the list(s). We doubt whether individual inspectors can, in practice, handle all the demands on them; each, as some of our informants told us, is likely to draw up their own 'approach', jeopardizing in the process the chances of consistency. We would seek to prune a good deal more regularly than has been the practice to date.

A little judicious pruning might bring some rewards but cuts on a larger scale would, in our view, be better. The Framework's aspiration to 'comprehensiveness' is the stumbling block here. Some elements of a school's functioning are undoubtedly more important than others and these should be reflected in the approach adopted. The four criteria relating to the identification of 'failing' schools already provide one example of such prioritizing. Although a 'full' inspection helps to expand the amount of information on which inspectors can base such a decision, we doubt whether all the information generated by a 'full' inspection is required. At the same time we would simplify the overall judgement to be made about a school's performance to a straightforward dichotomy. In one grouping would be all the schools which were either 'failing' or had 'serious weaknesses'; both need attention so it seems unnecessary to be particularly precise about the extent of difficulties. This group would contain a small minority of schools. The other would continue to be comprised of the much larger, essentially undifferentiated, remainder for whom different priorities in different cases might apply. An individual school would still be able to judge how well it had done from the kinds of issues which were recommended for its subsequent development.

The idea that an inspection takes place over a short period (usually a week) needs to be examined. Schools prepare for the 'inspection week' as a period of intensive interaction when they must do their best to 'perform' well but, at the same time, frequently claim that what the inspectors saw was not necessarily 'typical' of others parts of the school year. Such claims need to be recognized for the special pleading they sometimes represent. Nonetheless, we believe there is a case to be considered. We are not arguing that inspections should take place over considerably longer periods but the idea that a 'snapshot' of a school is the best way of identifying its strengths and weaknesses needs to be reconsidered. Some of the LEAs we studied had been exploring approaches along similar lines. A variety of consequences (some of them unfortunate) flow from the assumption that everything will be sorted out within the course of the single week. The pressure is on the inspectors to make their decisions quickly. They may be able to do this but schools in trouble may need more time, more reflection and, perhaps, a few more visits. Indeed, several of our interviewees complained about the lack of time for reflection before making their judgements. It is fairly easy to understand why a week may have seemed the right period when a team of HMI had to be brought together from around the country but with regionally-based inspection teams the same constraints on travelling patterns are unlikely to apply. A pattern which was probably dictated in the past by the need to coordinate the timetables of the Great Western and London, Midland & Scottish Railways should not be allowed to influence current procedures unduly.

The practice of only allowing schools to correct points of 'fact' prior to publication of the inspectors' final report needs to be modified. By their very nature judgements in education are contestable. By denying schools the 'right of reply' in the actual report both sides may be forced into positions they do not really want to maintain. The inspectors, for their part, may be inclined to 'pull their punches' whilst schools, frustrated by the lack of opportunity to put their side of the case, may set up strategies for discounting the validity of the inspectors' conclusions. One of the LEAs we studied made a deliberate point of requesting a commentary from the headteacher of the school they were inspecting for inclusion as an appendix to their public report. Schools should, we believe, be allowed to survive the process of inspection with their dignity shaken, perhaps, but still (largely) intact. If the inspectors' judgements are insufficiently 'robust' to survive the kinds of criticism which might ensue, then it might be questionable whether they merited serious attention anyway.

Finally, we would expect to build a clearer framework of performance indicators against which to judge different types of school. We do not believe that statistics alone can render an adequate picture of how well a school is doing. It continues to strike us as extraordinary, however, that inspectors still have to rely, in large measure, on their 'experience' to help them decide whether a school is achieving the kind of exam results one would predict from knowledge of its intake. Nor need such Frameworks be limited to exam or test results. Practice north of the border suggests that quite informative systems of 'indicators' can be built at relatively low cost (see McGlynn and Stalker 1995) and there are tentative signs that something might eventually emerge south of the border too. To their credit OFSTED commissioned a research study (Sammons *et al.* 1994) to help them set a broad framework for contextualizing schools' results; but, by their own admission, this was very much a first step. Meanwhile OFSTED inspection teams had undertaken well over a full year's worth of inspections without benefit of this sort of advice, not to mention the numerous inspectors practising in the pre-OFSTED era. The need for a strong statistical framework, whose strengths and weaknesses are understood by all concerned, remains paramount.

Strategies for enhancing the extent of school improvement

The research literature on factors contributing to school improvement is relatively well-established, unlike that on the effects of school inspection. Many factors have been identified which might be expected, depending on the position and circumstances of an individual school, to make a contribution. However, the research field has been dominated, in our view, by just three key concerns. The first of these is how to ensure greater 'ownership' of change initiatives amongst those most closely involved. The second is how to create greater 'focus' on the priorities that matter; change efforts which embrace wide-ranging objectives are hard to sustain. And the third relates to aspects of time; two to three years may be required for a specific initiative to take root and as long again for it to become institutionalized (see Gray and Wilcox 1995 for a lengthier   review).

A number of different strategies have been adopted by those in charge of inspection programmes to try to create a greater sense of ownership. In an earlier chapter we described some of the efforts different LEAs had made to involve schools and teachers in setting parts of the agenda for inspection as well as contributing, in some way or other, to the evidence-gathering. Some critics have suggested that greater sharing of assumptions and procedures is required (Hargreaves 1995). Headteachers, for example, might spend part of their time on secondment to inspection teams (Wragg and Brighouse 1995). Inspectors, indeed, might be required 'to spend at least a third of their time teaching in schools' (Hargreaves 1995).

Whilst this kind of sharing may be valuable in a general sort of way, it is not likely, in our view, to increase very dramatically feelings of ownership in the particular school being inspected. Of course, in certain circumstances any attempt to share perspectives and change feelings may be utopian. The only way we can see of this being tackled, however, is for someone the school 'trusts' being given some sort of role on the inspection team. Such a person is *likely* to be a member of the school's staff but not necessarily so; an 'outsider' could be nominated. Obviously objections might be made about the 'neutrality' of such a person or their possible influence on the ways in which the inspection team conducted their business; protocols about their contribution would need to be developed. Such an approach would, of course, run counter to current procedures whereby certain kinds of 'prior knowledge' of a school debar inspectors from further involvement. Before the idea is dismissed too readily, however, it might be worth noting that the Further Education Funding Council (whose model of inspection bears a strong resemblance in most other respects to those of other inspection agencies) has already gone some way down this road. A member of staff from the institution under review is made a temporary member of the inspection team (Melia 1995). This 'inspector' then participates at all stages up to (but not including) the one where specific judgements are made about the institution's gradings.

There is a danger that notions of 'ownership' may be neglected at other stages of the inspection process as well. 'Skilled observation', it was claimed, 'could throw into particularly sharp relief the highs and lows of pupils' school life – the magical, inspired or simply very competent lessons they experience as well as any moments of torpor, incomprehension or alienation' (Millett 1993). Descriptions of school practice which drew attention to such features could, indeed, serve as energizing forces. Millett is right, in our view, about the power of 'skilled observation' not only to produce these kinds of descriptions but also to generate insights into how they might be attained by others. The most credible part of this case, as far as teachers in a particular school are concerned, is likely to be the fact that the incidents were observed in *their* school. Unfortunately, we ourselves have yet to have the good fortune to read descriptions of such 'magical' or 'inspired' lessons in inspection reports. We have, of course, encountered numerous statements by inspectors to the effect that the teaching they observed was, in their opinion, 'very competent' – and quite a few where they were not so complimentary. The heart of the teaching and learning process is almost invariably missing from the descriptions that are presented. Indeed, we suspect that if the *Times Educational Supplement* were to call for examples from the previous six months' inspections there would be, at most, half a dozen entries – and there might not be any.

We have observed with interest the rise of planning processes to a central place in school improvement strategies. The need for a 'good plan' seems self-evident and certainly seems to offer a procedure for focusing a school's activities. Handled appropriately it can offer a means of bringing a number of potentially disparate strands of energy around a school into one coherent whole. We are mindful, however, of the history of school development planning (the forerunner of action planning) to date. Many schools have considerable difficulty in constructing plans which combine both the practicalities of organizing change efforts with the visions necessary to galvanize fresh energies (Hargreaves and Hopkins 1994). And even when they have constructed what looks, on paper, like a 'good plan', few plans have the power to withstand the battering daily exposure to school life can bring. As MacGilchrist and colleagues (1995) have shown, some are simply rhetorical exercises, some have their heart in the right place but not a great deal else, and only a handful seem capable of improving students' learning, if anyone were to hang around long enough to find out. OFSTED's own study (1995d) of schools' action plans has demonstrated something rather similar. Hardly any schools had developed lines of thinking through to the bitter end of the improvement process by setting 'specific targets for the improvement of achievement' or 'develop[ing] criteria or indicators against which to monitor or evaluate the effectiveness of the proposed action in terms of raised standards'. As the study put it these are the 'acid tests' of the school's strategies.

There is also a counter-trend in some of the literature. One of the pieces of advice from Louis and Miles' (1992) study of disadvantaged urban high schools seeking to improve that sticks with us is that they should 'do and then plan'. Anything, they seem to be saying, that can get *some* action going is worth contemplating. Start, in short, where the staff are – the planning can come later. In brief, we are arguing that the central problem is to get the school to focus on something but that the means should not be too readily prescribed. In some schools all that may be required are refinements to planning processes which are already in place. Other schools may be less fortunate. Planning processes which are capable of delivering real change may not be in place. In such circumstances to concentrate on 'the plans' may be diversionary.

The difficulties schools might experience in planning change are one part of a much larger problem which those who would bring about improvement through inspection have to face. The concern with how things are now (during the inspection week) has somehow deflected attention away from how things were or how things might be. Several heads in our study, feeling wounded by comments inspectors had made about their schools' performance, were of the view that more attention should have been paid to how much the school had already achieved (in most cases since they took over). Such assessments occasionally surface in the pages of final reports but they are usually brief. Yet surely the best prognosis of whether a school will improve in the future is some assessment of how much it has been improving in the past?

In our view there has been a missing section in inspection manuals over the years. At the same time as asking questions about what a school needs to do in order to improve inspectors should have been asking equally searching questions about what a school has *already* done. As Hargreaves (1995: 123) has observed, 'Inspection is a form of *quality control* and the trouble with quality control is that it merely monitors the failure rate or the site of failure but does nothing itself to put the fault right. Japanese industry has succeeded in part because it dropped quality control in favour of *quality assurance*, which returns to the workforce the responsibility for quality.'

We ourselves would term this 'missing section' the school's 'capacity to improve'. A whole bundle of factors, which are currently spread around the manual in a disconnected sort of way, are likely to be relevant. Evidence is usually collected, for example, on teachers' expectations, on management styles across and within departments, on the extent of collaborative planning and on staff development strategies. Comparisons of the school's performance with previous years are also sometimes made (although the most frequent comparison is typically only with last year). But no one seems to have given much attention to the task of bringing all these disparate sources together and asking the crunch question: 'Is this school on an upward trajectory?' Our assessment of such little evidence as is available on this subject also leads us to doubt whether this 'capacity' is evenly distributed across schools or widely available (see Gray *et al.* 1996b). It is particularly likely to be absent from schools in trouble. In many more instances, however, the first recommendation for action should surely be that the school starts to build this 'capacity'. But how could the school know this if the inspectors have omitted to comment on it?

Our final concern relates to time and timing. An inspection report can be an effective means of creating a sense of urgency that something needs to be done. The situations it describes, however, are quite likely to be deeply rooted and longstanding. There is something portentous about the 40 days which schools are given to come up with action plans which may, again, contribute to the sense of urgency. But after that, except in the case of schools in serious difficulties, life usually returns to 'normal'. The sense of urgency begins to diminish and other priorities are likely to force their ways onto the agenda. Inspectors (or acquaintances of the inspectors) may return in some other guise to support the action but their time is very limited.

Keeping up the impetus almost invariably becomes a problem as memories of the inspection begin to fade. Schools have their own 'natural histories' of change which those who would improve ignore at their peril. In some (a minority we suspect) improvement is a steady process – successive hurdles are identified and got over by one means or another. Post-inspection monitoring of targets will probably yield worthwhile evidence. Others (the majority) probably go in fits and starts – hurdles are identified and some are got over but the patterns are uneven. What a short-term post-inspection follow-up will yield is likely to be patchy and unconvincing. Across-the-board assumptions, therefore, about how long change takes are likely to be inappropriate; this will vary from school to school. We share the view that 'failing' schools should not hang around or, for that matter, be permitted to do so. Such limited evidence as we have available, however, suggests that really worthwhile changes (that is changes in schools' 'effectiveness' as institutions) will take years rather than months. Three or four years will probably be required for an 'ineffective' school to move into the pack and as long again for it to move ahead (see Gray *et al.* 1996b; and the follow-up study conducted by Louis and Miles 1992).

Given the complexities and vagaries of the change process, how might inspectors take the time dimension on board? The easiest way would be to use the next inspection (five years later in our plan) partly for this purpose, using the earlier inspection report as a baseline. Such a development would, of course, pose new challenges for current inspection practices but not, we suspect, insurmountable ones.

Changes in OFSTED's approach

In the old days, before the advent of OFSTED, the inspection manual was a fairly closely guarded secret. Bits of it were shared, on occasion, in an informal way and parts surfaced, once in a while, as appendices to various national surveys. One of the advantages of having an inspection process based on a manual which is publicly available is that all those involved in the activity (inspectors and the inspected) can debate and suggest changes. OFSTED has adopted an unusually open attitude (for a government department) in this respect. It came as no surprise, therefore, to learn that as we were completing the manuscript for this book in the Autumn of 1995 OFSTED published the results of the consultation process on the proposed revisions of the Framework which had been circulated earlier in the year (OFSTED 1995f). As a result a new Framework and Handbook (in three separate versions for primary, secondary and special schools) have been produced for implementation in the summer of 1996 (OFSTED 1995g; 1995h; 1995i). Much of this bodes well for the future.

Two major aims of the revision were to make inspection more manageable for inspectors and to reduce the burden on schools. The Handbooks have been slimmed down to about half the former size although their structure, and much of their content, are the same. There are several significant modifications to the model of the school as we interpreted it in earlier chapters.[2] There is a more explicit recognition of the context of a school and reports are to include a brief statement of the main aims and priorities of schools and any targets set or adopted.

'Standards of achievement' has been retitled 'attainment and progress' and requires pupils' progress to be judged in relation to prior attainment rather than, as in the earlier versions, to ability. It is difficult to see, however, how this change of terminology makes the inspectors' task of forming judgements in this area easier or more secure. 'Attainment and progress' is one of the three main outcomes specified; the others are 'attitudes, behaviour and personal development' and 'attendance' (included in the 1994 edition as a 'contributory factor'). 'Quality of learning' disappears as a separate entity for judgement although important aspects of learning (skills and attitudes) will still be reported. The quasi-causal 'contributory factors' have been regrouped, and in some cases combined (e.g. curriculum and assessment, equal opportunities and special needs), under the main report headings of 'quality of education provided' or the 'management and efficiency of the school'.

Meanwhile the actual inspection process remains essentially unchanged although the number of evaluation criteria to be observed in making judgements has been substantially reduced. Judgements, however, will now be rated on seven-point scales instead of five. Some moves have also been made towards a more developmental form of inspection. Key issues are to be prioritized according to their importance in improving pupils' attainment. The report will, at the same time, acknowledge if a key issue has been identified as a priority in the school's development plan.

On into the future?

The last few years have witnessed a significant policy initiative in education – swiftly implemented and with ambitious objectives. Unlike crude 'league tables' of schools' results and other rather simplistic forms of holding schools to account, inspection offers the prospect of an 'enlightened view' of the nature and purposes of schooling. The possibility that it might also serve as a means of school improvement provides a potentially potent combination. It is not surprising therefore that other countries have awaited the outcomes of the 'British experiment' with considerable interest.

Nonetheless there is a paradox at the centre of the reform process. Inspection has undoubtedly changed more in the last five years than for most of its previous lengthy tradition – or at least the arrangements for organizing it have changed. The core methodology, however, remains stubbornly familiar. History tells us that institutions which have been built to secure greater accountability do not usually succeed in embracing other purposes as well. Fortunately for those who would 'improve through inspection', history is not an exact science and benefits considerably from the wisdom of hindsight.

APPENDIX:

INSPECTIONS STUDIED

LEA	School*	Type of inspection				
		Part	Full	Supported self-evaluation	Pilot OFSTED	OFSTED
Mortdale	High Lees Primary	x				
	St Peter's Junior		x			
	Ecclesley Secondary (11–16)				x	
	Monkton Secondary (11–16)		x			
Falton	Richardson Primary				x	
	Murbank Primary				x	
	Prince Edward Secondary (11–16)				x	
	Laurels Secondary (11–16)				x	
Churdley	Danbrook Primary	x				
	Playfair Primary				x	
	Midchester Secondary (11–16)				x	
	Tennyson Road Secondary (11–16)	x				

LEA	School*	Type of inspection				
		Part	Full	Supported self-evaluation	Pilot OFSTED	OFSTED
Forestshire	Low Springs Primary		x			
	Milton Primary		x			
	Carlow Secondary (11–18)		x			
	Alderman King Secondary (11–18)				x	
Sedley	Fenby Junior	x		x		
	Lowstone Primary	x		x		
	Turner Secondary (11–16)	x		x		
Folkshire	Austin Road Primary		x			
	St Mark's Middle		x			
	Potterton Secondary (11–16)				x	
	Strafford High School (11–16)		x			
Middleshire	Trenton Storrs Middle		x			
Besford	Coverley Junior					x
	Broad Lane Primary					x
	Low Moors Secondary (11–18)					x
	Ladywell Secondary (11–18)					x
Loamshire	Burnden Special School					x
Totals		6	9	3	9	5

* Names of schools have been changed to protect identities.

NOTES

Chapter 1: Inspection: promises and challenges

1 The Education Act (1944) had given LEAs the right to inspect their schools. In practice, inspections were generally carried out by specialist staff appointed by LEAs and variously termed 'inspectors' or 'advisers'.

2 Readers may not be aware that some care needs to be exercised in referring to the areas of Britain which were affected by the reforms. England and Wales were exposed to the new OFSTED regime. Wales, in fact, has a separate system, albeit one which closely mirrors that for England. In general it is the arrangements for England which are described here. In Scotland, however, HM Inspectorate were retained although there were some changes in their approach (see McGlynn and Stalker 1995 for a more detailed account and McPherson and Raab 1988 for a fuller history of the Scottish Inspectorate's influence on the system). Some care is also needed when referring to the different sectors of education. The model of inspection adopted by the Further Education Funding Council departs in several key respects from that adopted by OFSTED (see Melia 1995 for fuller details).

3 The schools covered are all maintained schools including self-governing, grant-maintained schools, city technology colleges and independent schools in receipt of government funds.

4 Frost's observations about the literature on school effectiveness (and, we assume, school improvement) prompted us to look with a fresh eye at Michael Fullan's (1991) usually authoritative account of the research on school change and improvement. The word 'inspection' does not occur in the index although 'monitoring' and other related concepts do. We noted that the concept of 'pressure' (which occurs frequently in discussions of the probable impact of inspections) is not indexed either although it appears at some points during discussion of the related concept of 'support'. Some of the problems that are likely to stem from governments' attempts to secure 'compliance' with their policies are referred to at greater length. The concept of 'pressure' is not indexed either in Fullan's (1992) later study. Again the concept of 'support'

carries the weight of the argument with a short section on the importance of 'integrating authority and support' getting nearest to the 'pressure' component of the change process. Fullan does, however, say that one should: 'assume that people need pressure to change (even in directions that they desire)', but that such efforts will 'be effective only under conditions that allow them to react, to form their own position, to interact with other implementors, to obtain external assistance, etc' (1991: 106).

5 OFSTED, for example, has a Quality Assurance and Development section which has commissioned various studies into the functioning of inspection (see Matthews, 1995).

6 Various aspects of the history of school evaluation up to the end of the 1980s have been covered by Silver (1994).

7 The study looked at practices in England, France, Germany, New Zealand, Spain, Sweden and the United States of America.

8 One of us has attempted in the past to tease out what kind of evaluation model inspection most closely approximates to. 'Connoisseurship' seems the most likely answer (Wilcox 1989).

9 Interestingly, this concern was widely-voiced after HM Inspectorate had conducted a national survey of primary schools in the late 1970s (DES 1978).

10 See Chapter 3 of Gray and Wilcox (1995) for a fuller account of the efforts made by HMI over the better part of a decade to come up with more appropriate strategies for contextualizing schools' performance.

11 Brimblecombe and colleagues (1995b) have argued that teachers take 'attitudes' of inspectors into account in deciding which proposals to respond to.

12 The figure of £30,000 per secondary school inspected was widely quoted during 1992 when tendering for inspection contracts was being discussed. Competitive tendering may have reduced the costs a little since then. Obviously the sums for individual primary schools would be much less than those for the average secondary.

13 The 'distinguished researchers' cited include: Brian Caldwell, Peter Cuttance, Michael Fullan, Michael Huberman, Karen Seashore Lewis, Matthew Miles and Jaap Scheerens.

14 See chapters by Jesson and Reynolds, Reynolds and Gray in Gray *et al.* (1996b) and Chapter 12 of Gray and Wilcox (1995) for extended discussions of the debates about the 'ineffective' schools.

15 *The Times* reported that all but one of the schools identified as 'failing' had been reprieved (3 April 1995). The same paper noted that 'a target of two years for most schools has been set' (4 April 1995).

Chapter 2: Schools under the microscope: three case studies

1 The total sample of case studies consisted of inspections of primary and secondary schools in seven LEAs. The cases were originally chosen to represent the different approaches adopted by LEAs to inspection in the pre-OFSTED period. The case studies were part of a larger project, funded by the Economic and Social Research Council, called Programmes to Assess the Quality of Schooling (PAQS) carried out over the period 1991–4. As a consequence of the passing of the Education (Schools) Act 1992 during this period some of the later inspections were carried out using the OFSTED Framework. The sample was subsequently extended to include five OFSTED inspections from a further two LEAs. The Appendix gives details of the full range of inspections studied.

2 Individual, semi-structured interviews were conducted for each inspection with

samples of the teaching staff and the inspection team. The samples included the headteacher, usually the deputy headteacher, and the inspection team leader. From four to six other teachers and two to four other inspectors were also usually interviewed. The aim was to elicit individual reactions to the inspection process and its findings. Interviews took about 45 minutes, were tape recorded for subsequent analysis, and were carried out, where possible, after the draft inspection report had been prepared and/or findings fed back to the school staff.

Interviews were supplemented, where posssible by opportunities to observe the planning and the conduct of pre-inspection and post-inspection activities.

In the full study of which the three inspections of Chapter 2 are only a part, follow up interviews were carried out some nine to 12 months later (and also a further six to nine months on in the case of the secondary school inspections). This second level of data, which is specifically concerned with the effects of the inspection on the school's subsequent development will be considered in more detail in Chapter 7.

3 LEAs usually designated a specific inspector, variously termed 'school inspector', 'link inspector', 'pastoral inspector' for each of their schools. Such inspectors were expected to get to know the schools and their staff by maintaining a programme of regular visits. They were generally envisaged as a school's first source of general advice. Although they were sometimes involved in the inspection of their schools this would now be precluded under OFSTED arrangements.

4 Where a selected pupil is followed by an inspector throughout the school day to generate a series of lessons for observation.

5 Before the introduction of the OFSTED inspection programme in September 1993 a programme of inspections was carried out during the previous year by HMI using the OFSTED Framework. These inspections served the important purpose of providing a training opportunity for LEA inspectors and others seeking to become inspectors for OFSTED in the future. These 'HMI' teams therefore typically consisted of a number of 'trainee' inspectors.

Chapter 3: The origins and development of school inspection

1 The National Society (full name: the National Society for Promoting the Education of the Poor in the Principles of the Established Church) was a Church of England organization and the British and Foreign Schools Society was concerned with interdenominational schools.

2 This committee was the first body to oversee the emerging system of public education. It was succeeded over the years by the Education Department, the Board of Education, the Ministry of Education, the Department of Education and Science (DES) and most recently by the Department for Education (DFE) and the Department for Education and Employment (DFEE).

3 This survey was part of our PAQS project.

4 'Part' inspection was our name for those inspections concerned with some of the main aspects of a school, i.e. less comprehensive in coverage than 'full' inspections. Part inspections refer to those inspections often called 'short' inspections by HMI and others.

5 These two studies are difficult to compare directly because different measures were used for the extent or volume of inspection.

6 Reported in *Education*, 17 May 1991: 389.

7 See the comments of Councillor Sams, Conservative chairman of Bexley's education committee reported in *Education*, 9 August 1991: 101.

Chapter 4: The claims for inspection

1 In OFSTED inspections this leadership role is performed by the Registered Inspector (RgI).
2 Early HM inspectors were appointed from the educated 'upper' classes (often clerics) and were thus socially and culturally different from the elementary school teachers they inspected.
3 A lay inspector is defined as a person 'without personal experience in the management of any school or the provision of education in any school (otherwise than as a governor or in any other voluntary capacity) . . .' (DES 1992a: 17).
4 The 1992 Act states that no member of an inspection team is allowed to have a connection with the school, its staff or governors which casts doubt upon his or her ability to report impartially upon it. Thus an LEA inspector can be ruled out if there has been a close working relationship with the school in question that might cast doubts on the inspector's ability to report impartially upon it (DFE 1993a).
5 The highest proportion of the early inspections (77.3 per cent) went to LEA inspection teams. This proportion had fallen to 52.2 per cent by the summer of 1994 as contracts were increasingly awarded to non-LEA contractors (Matthews and Smith 1995).
6 The remit of an education association is to 'bring experienced management and leadership to ensure that the problems identified in the inspection report are remedied' (DFE 1993a). The school remains under the control of the association until a subsequent inspection shows that 'special measures' are no longer required. At that point the association is required to seek grant-maintained status for the school. This will be decided by the Secretary of State in the usual way. The school will not return to its former maintaining authority.
7 The 1994 version of the Handbook has pages numbered consecutively from one onwards within each major section. As a result, references are indicated by section and page, for example, (3) 13–14.
8 We draw here and elsewhere on results (both published and unpublished) of our survey of LEAs (Wilcox et al. 1993) referred to in Chapter 3.
9 This comment was made by the new CI some 18 months after our first interview with the previous incumbent. By that time a new CEO was also in post and a new culture was being established.
10 Given that the method of questioning was open-ended, it should not be inferred too readily that because something was not mentioned it did not occur.
11 Advisory teachers were appointed, increasingly on short-term contracts, to support teachers in specific curriculum or other specialist areas. They provided in-service activities and might also work with teachers directly in the classroom.
12 The metaphor of 'family resemblances' has been developed more fully by Wittgenstein (1958: 66–7).

Chapter 5: The experience of inspection: pressures and anxieties

1 With the onset of OFSTED inspections, articles have appeared in the educational press in which schools have described their experience of being inspected. An example of the growth of postgraduate theses is provided by the output of a recent MEd course for LEA inspectors organized by the University of Sheffield and the Centre for Adviser and Inspector Development.
2 The case studies constitute the third and major aspect of our PAQS project to which reference has previously been made.
3 Although the LEA identified four potential evaluations for study our negotiations

with the headteacher of one of the schools involved were unsuccessful. Researching individual inspections can be a sensitive issue for schools and their reluctance to be involved in what may seem to be further interventions into their normal routines is understandable. We were in fact somewhat surprised that we did not encounter similar reluctance in the other schools which we approached.

4 In most schools we interviewed the headteacher, the deputy most closely involved in the inspection, and a random selection of heads of department (or subject coordinators in primary schools) and classroom teachers. In most cases the total sample ranged from four to nine staff. In two inspections, however, we were only granted interviews with the headteacher (Laurels Secondary School) and with the headteacher and deputy (Richardson Primary School).

5 The follow-up interviews provide the empirical basis of Chapter 7.

6 See note 3, Chapter 2.

7 See note 4, Chapter 2.

8 Cuts in government grants to LEAs and the limitations imposed on them for raising funds locally have resulted in reductions in advisory and support services. In addition, as a consequence of the 1992 Act, engagement in post-inspection support of specific schools could render inspectors ineligible for future inspections of those schools.

9 See for example the article of inspector Bill Graham 'Falling asleep on the job' (*Education*, 10 March 1995, p. 10).

Chapter 6: The methodological problems of inspection

1 At the time of writing a new version of the Framework has gone out for consultation. The aim is to reduce the demands made on schools and to make the process of inspection more manageable for inspectors. This has been undertaken in response particularly to the experience of headteachers of primary schools inspected in the Autumn term 1994. New versions of the Framework and Handbook were introduced in 1995 for implementation in summer 1996.

2 The prototype is the Flanders (1970) Interaction Analysis Categories (FIAC) which code different categories of teacher and pupil talk. The categories are termed 'low inference' because they can be 'objectively' ascribed to aspects of talk without requiring much in the way of inference from the observer. Examples from the 'teacher talk' category of FIAC include: 'asking questions', 'giving directions', 'lecturing'.

3 High inference categories identify more general or complex aspects of talk or behaviour where the observer's inference or judgement is more crucial (see p. 72).

4 Unlike the five-point scales used in classroom observation, the mid-point of the seven-point scales of JRSs is 'where there is a balance between the two descriptors, an equal measure of strengths and weaknesses and is not the point on the scale equating to terms such as "satisfactory" or "average"' (OFSTED 1994b: (3) 59). Some inspectors reported experiencing difficulty in converting gradings from five-point to seven-point scales.

5 The definition of 'satisfactory' for point 3 on the scale has now been replaced by 'sound' (OFSTED 1994b: (3) 16).

Chapter 7: The impact of inspection on schools' development

1 See note 4, Chapter 5.

2 It had been our intention to interview the inspector sample used in the first set of interviews. It soon became apparent however that, in almost all cases, the only

inspector who had any detailed knowledge of post-inspection developments was the school inspector. Even school inspectors found it difficult, given their many commitments, to maintain post-inspection contact with their schools.

3 Interviews lasted approximately 45 minutes and were recorded. The resulting tapes were used to supplement brief notes taken during the interview. The process resulted in the production of substantial summaries organized initially in terms of the responses of individual interviewees to each question. A series of categories was then derived inductively by scrutinizing these summaries. The categories provided a basis for presenting the results in the form of matrices of a kind similar to those proposed by Miles and Huberman (1984). The tables in this chapter were in turn derived from these matrices and constituted a final stage of data reduction.

4 We are grateful to our colleague Dr Pamela Poppleton for carrying out the fieldwork for this inspection.

5 In April 1993, the Secretary of State for Education invited Sir Ron Dearing to review the structure, manageability and assessment arrangements of the National Curriculum. See SCAA (1994).

6 OFSTED's own research would seem to support this conclusion. No fewer than 96 per cent of the 85 schools visited had 'addressed all of the key issues from the inspection' in their action plans and 91 per cent had also 'made adequate preparation for their action plans, which in a third of schools enabled work to begin on the plan before receipt of the published report. A lower but still high proportion (84 per cent) had set out a clear timetable and identified the person responsible for each aspect'. Three fifths (61 per cent) had made 'discernible progress at an early stage in tackling some of the key issues in a way which was leading to, or likely to lead to, improvement by taking measures to improve teaching, raise expectations, address underachievement or ensure that pupils had more positive attitudes to their work'.

Overall the study seems to yield a similar picture to our own. But interpretations regarding the extent of similarity with our own findings hang, of course, on what is meant by 'discernible progress'. The survey does not state exactly how long the gap between the inspections (which occurred throughout 1993/4) and the inspectors' follow-up visits actually was; it seems likely that the nearest equivalent was our nine- to 12-month follow-up.

As regards 'acid tests' the findings were very similar to our own. Few schools (only 4 per cent) had 'set specific targets for improvement of achievement'; and few (8 per cent) had 'developed criteria or indicators against which to monitor and evaluate the effectiveness of the proposed action in terms of raised standards' (OFSTED 1995d: 3–4).

Chapter 8: Inspection and the case of the 'failing' school

1 The provisions on failing schools in the 1992 Act (Schedule 2, para 11) refer to a school considered to be 'at risk', defined as ' . . . failing or . . . likely to fail, to give its pupils an acceptable standard of education . . . '. In the 1993 Act the term 'at risk' has been replaced by 'requiring special measures'.

2 At the time of our interview the acting headteacher had become the former acting headteacher. However, we continue to use the title 'acting headteacher' to avoid confusion.

3 A grant maintained school (GMS), being one which is funded directly by the DFE, is outside the control of an LEA and its services to schools.

4 As we anticipated, however, schools in difficulties had more trouble drawing up plans. The OFSTED study states (1995d: 4): 'schools with serious weaknesses, but not

formally identified as requiring special measures, did not receive sufficient support (from their LEAs or other bodies) to produce an effective action plan'. 'Failing' schools did get this kind of help from their LEAs, the study reports.

Chapter 9: Some theoretical perspectives on inspection

1 The practice of including a member of staff in an inspection team is a recognized feature of the inspection arrangements applying to the further education service (see Melia 1995).
2 For details of Jeremy Bentham's *panopticon* see Foucault (1977: 200 *et seq*).
3 Habermas devotes little attention to the nature of education generally and certainly none to inspection.

Chapter 10: Looking to the future

1 The full programme announced by Gillian Shephard, Secretary of State for Education on 25 May 1995 consisted of: the establishment of a DFE team to include the HMCI, the Chief Executive of the Teacher Training Agency and the Director of the University of London Institute of Education; a study to identify schools which were setting targets and using them to raise standards; a grant payable to all schools on submission of their post-inspection plans; inspectors revisiting all schools identified as having serious weaknesses; a review of INSET; action to identify good teaching methods and improve teachers' effectiveness; the formation of an advisory group for improving schools; and an OECD conference to share international experiences on school improvement (DFE 1995).
2 The three versions of the Handbook have the same model of the school. Its characteristics may be summarized in terms of:

Outcomes (educational standards achieved)
Attainment and progress
Attitudes, behaviour and personal development
Attendance

and

Contributory factors
Provision   – Teaching
                   Curriculum and assessment
                   Pupils' spiritual, moral, social and cultural development
                   Support, guidance and pupils' welfare
                   Partnership with parents and the community
Management   – Leadership and management
                   Staffing, accommodation and learning resources
                   Efficiency of the school

Particular emphasis is to be given to 'attainment and progress', 'teaching' and 'leadership and management'.

(adapted from OFSTED (1995h: 42)

REFERENCES

Audit Commission (1989) *Assuring Quality in Education*. London: HMSO.

Baker, K. (1988) *Secretary of State's Speech to the Society of Education Officers, 22 January 1988*. London: Press Office, DES.

Ball, S. J. (ed.) (1990) *Foucault and Education*. London: Routledge.

Ball, S. J. (1994) *Education Reform: A Practical and Post-Structural Approach*. Buckingham: Open University Press.

Barnes, A. (1983) Undergoing a formal inspection – what it was like. *Education*, 20 May: 391–2.

Barnes, A. (1984) HMI inspection: what happens next? *Education*, 28 September: 257–8.

Blackie, J. (1982) HM Inspectorate of Schools 1839–1966, in R. McCormick and D. L. Nuttall (eds) *Curriculum Evaluation and Assessment in Educational Institutions*. Milton Keynes: The Open University.

Bolam, R., Smith, G. and Canter, H. (1978) *LEA Advisers and the Mechanisms of Innovation*. Windsor: NFER Nelson.

Brighouse, T. and Moon, R. (eds) (1995) *School Inspection*. London: Pitmans Publishing.

Brimblecombe, N., Ormston, M. and Shaw, M. (1995a) 'Teachers' Perceptions of School Inspection: a stressful experience'. *Cambridge Journal of Education*, 25, 1: 53–61.

Brimblecombe, N., Ormston, M. and Shaw, M. (1995b) Modified tactics. *Education*, 23 June: 12.

Broadbent, J., Laughlin, R. and Read, S. (1991) Recent financial and administrative changes in the NHS: a critical theory analysis. *Critical Perspectives on Accounting*, 2: 1–29.

Brooks, C. St. J. and Hirsch, D. (1995) *Schools under Scrutiny: Strategies for the Evaluation of School Performance*, Paris: Centre for Educational Research and Innovation, Organization for Economic Co-operation and Development.

Burchill, J. (1991a) Inspection that's worth the money, *Times Educational Supplement*, 14 June: 16.

Burchill, J. (1991b) *Inspecting Schools: Breaking the Monopoly*. London: Centre for Policy Studies.

Burchill, J. (1993) HMI Monopoly Marches On, *Guardian Education*, 26 January: 3.

Burchill, J. (1995) School inspection: who hath measured the ground? *Cambridge Journal of Education*, 25, 1: 109–16.

Cabinet Office (1991) *The Citizen's Charter: Raising the Standard*, Cmnd. 1599. London: HMSO.

Caldwell, B. J. and Spinks, J. M. (1988) *The Self-Managing School*. London: Falmer Press.

Caldwell, B. J. and Spinks, J. M. (1992) *Leading the Self-Managing School*. London: Falmer Press.

Clare, J. (1994) How to waste 112 million pounds, *Daily Telegraph*, 6 July.

Clift, P. S., Nuttall, D. L. and McCormick, R. (1987) *Studies in School Self-Evaluation*. London: Falmer Press.

Cox, C. B. and Dyson A. E. (eds) (1969a) *Fight for Freedom: A Black Paper*. London: The Critical Quarterly Society.

Cox, C. B. and Dyson A. E. (eds) (1969b) *Black Paper Two: The Crisis in Education*. London: The Critical Quarterly Society.

Cox, C. B. and Dyson A. E. (eds) (1970) *Black Paper Three: Goodbye Mr Short*. London: The Critical Quarterly Society.

Day, P. and Klein, R. (1987) *Accountabilities*. London: Tavistock.

DES (1968) *Report of Parliamentary Select Committee: Part I Her Majesty's Inspectorate*. London: HMSO.

DES (1977) *Education in Schools: A Consultative Document*, Cmnd 6869. London: HMSO.

DES (1978) *Primary Education in England: A Survey by HMI*. London: HMSO.

DES (1979) *Aspects of Secondary Education in England: A Survey by HMI*. London: HMSO.

DES (1985a) *Better Schools* (A White Paper), Cmnd. 9469. London: HMSO.

DES (1985b) *A Draft Statement on the Role of Local Advisory Services*. London: HMSO.

DES (1986) *Reporting Inspections: Maintained Schools*. London: DES.

DES (1988a) *Education Support Grant*, draft circular. London: DES.

DES (1988b) *The Education Reform Act 1988*. London: HMSO.

DES (1989) *The Education Support Grants (Amendment) Regulations 1989*, SI No. 2446. London: HMSO.

DES (1991a) *The Parent's Charter: You and Your Child's Education*. London: DES.

DES (1991b) *Launch of the Parent's Charter by the Secretary of State, 27 September 1991*. London: Press Office, DES.

DES (1992a) *Education (Schools) Act*. London: HMSO.

DES (1992b) *Education in England 1990–91: The Annual Report of HM Senior Chief Inspector of Schools*. London: DES.

DES/WO (1982) *Study of HM Inspectorate in England and Wales (Rayner Report)*. London: HMSO.

DFE (1992a) *Choice and Diversity: A New Framework for Schools* (A White Paper), Cmnd, 2021. London: HMSO.

DFE (1992b) *Draft Framework for the Inspection of Schools*. London: DFE.

DFE (1993a) *Inspecting Schools: A Guide to the Inspection Provisions of the Education (Schools) Act 1992*. Circular 7/93. London: DFE.

DFE (1993b) *The Education (School Inspection) (No 2) Regulations 1993*, SI No 1986. London: HMSO.

DFE (1995) Shephard launches school standards action plan. *Department for Education News* 11/95, 25 May.

Earley, P., Fidler, B. and Ouston, J. (1995) Secondary heads fear planning plight, *Times Educational Supplement*, p. 10, 6 January.

Education (1991) 17 May: 389.

Eisner, E . W. (1991) *The Enlightened Eye*. New York: Macmillan.

Elliott, J. and Ebbutt D. (1986) How do Her Majesty's Inspectors judge educational quality? *Curriculum*, 7, 3: 130–40.

Fitz-Gibbon, C. T. (1995) Ofsted, Schmofsted, in T. Brighouse and R. Moon (eds) *School Inspection*. London: Pitmans Publishing.

Flanders, N. A. (1970) *Analysing Teacher Behaviour*. New York: Addison-Wesley.

Foucault, M. (1977) *Discipline and Punishment: the Birth of the Prison*, 1991 edition. London: Penguin Press.

Frost, R. (1995) *Improvement Through Inspection*, briefing paper 9. London: National Commission on Education.

Fullan, M. (1982) *The Meaning of Educational Change*. New York: Teachers College Press.

Fullan, M. (1991) *The New Meaning of Educational Change*. London: Cassell.

Fullan, M. (1992) *Successful School Improvement: The Implementation Perspective and Beyond*. Buckingham: Open University Press.

Fullan, M. and Hargreaves, A. (1992) *What's Worth Fighting For in Your School? Working Together for Improvement*. Buckingham: Open University Press.

Gogol, N. (1987) *The Government Inspector*, Trans. D. J. Campbell. London: Heinemann.

Gray, J. and Hannon, V. (1986) HMI's interpretations of schools' examination results. *Journal of Education Policy*, 1, 1: 23–33.

Gray, J., Goldstein, H. and Jesson, D. (1996a) Changes and improvements in schools' effectiveness: trends over five years. *Research Papers in Education*, 11, 1.

Gray, J., Reynolds, D., Fitz-Gibbon, C. T. and Jesson, D. (eds)(1996b) *Merging Traditions: The Future of Research on School Effectiveness and School Improvement*. London: Cassell.

Gray, J. and Wilcox, B. (1995) *'Good School, Bad School': Evaluating Performance and Encouraging Improvement*. Buckingham: Open University Press.

HMI (1988a) *Inspection and Reporting*. Working Notes for HMI. London: DES.

HMI (1988b) *Rating Scales and HMI Exercises*. Working Notes for HMI. London: DES.

Habermas, J. (1982) Reply to my critics, in J. B. Thompson and D. Held (eds) *Habermas: Critical Debates*, p. 266.

Habermas, J. (1984) *The Theory of Communicative Action: Reason and Rationalisation of Society*. Cambridge: Polity Press.

Habermas, J. (1987) *The Theory of Communicative Action: The Critique of Functionalist Reason*. Cambridge: Polity Press.

Hargreaves, A. (1994) *Changing Teachers, Changing Times: Teachers' Work and Culture in the Postmodern Age*. London: Cassell.

Hargreaves, D. H. (1990) Accountability and school improvement in the work of LEA inspectors: the rhetoric and beyond. *Journal of Education Policy*, 5, 3: 230–9.

Hargreaves, D. H. (1995) Inspection and school improvement. *Cambridge Journal of Education*, 25, 1: 117–25.

Hargreaves, D. H. and Hopkins, D. (1991) *The Empowered School: The Management and Practice of Development Planning*. London: Cassell.

Hargreaves, D. H. and Hopkins, D. (eds) (1994) *Development Planning for School Improvement*. London: Cassell.

Henkel, M. (1991) *Government, Evaluation and Change*. London: Jessica Kingsley.

Hohengarten, W. H. (1992) Translator's introduction, in J. Habermas, *Postmetaphysical Thinking*, pp. viii–xi. Cambridge: Polity Press.

Jones, L. and Moore, R. (1995) Appropriating competence: the competency movement, the New Right and the 'culture change' project. *British Journal of Education and Work*, 8, 2: 78–92.

Kogan, M. (1986) *Education Accountability: An Analytic Overview*. London: Routledge and Kegan Paul.

Lawlor, S. (1993) *Inspecting the School Inspectors: New Plans, Old Ills*. London: Centre for Policy Studies.

Lawton, D. and Gordon, P. (1987) *HMI*. London: Routledge and Kegan Paul.

Lincoln, Y. S. and Guba, E. G. (1985) *Naturalistic Enquiry*. Beverly Hills: Sage.

Louis, K. S. and Miles, M. B. (1992) *Improving the Urban High School: What Works and Why*. London: Cassell.

Maclure, J. S. (1969) *Educational Documents: England and Wales, 1816–1968*. London: Methuen.

Matthews, P. (1995) Aspects of inspection, improvement and OFSTED, in T. Brighouse and B. Moon (eds) *School Inspection*. London: Pitman Publishing.

Matthews, P. and Smith, G. (1995) OFSTED: Inspecting schools and improvement through inspection. *Cambridge Journal of Education*, 25, 1: 23–34.

Maw, J. (1995) The *Handbook for the Inspection of Schools*: a critique. *Cambridge Journal of Education*, 25, 1: 75–87.

Maychell, K. and Keys, W. (1993) *LEA Evaluation and Monitoring*. Slough: NFER.

MacGilchrist, B., Mortimore, P., Savage, J. and Beresford, C. (1995) *Planning Matters*. London: Paul Chapman.

McGlynn, A. and Stalker, H. (1995) Recent developments in the Scottish process of school inspection. *Cambridge Journal of Education*, 25, 1: 13–21.

McPherson, A. F. and Raab, C. D. (1988) *Governing Education: A Sociology of Policy since 1945*. Edinburgh: Edinburgh University Press.

Melia, T. P. (1995) Quality and its assurance in further education. *Cambridge Journal of Education*, 25, 1: 35–44.

Miles, M. B. and Huberman, A. (1984) *Qualitative Analysis*. London: Sage.

Miles, W. J. W. (1982) *The Inspectorial Role of HMI with a Case Study Analysis of the Full Inspection*. MEd dissertation. University of Birmingham.

Millett, A. (1993) How inspectors can actually help, *Times Educational Supplement*, 25 June.

Nebesnuick, D. (1991) *Promoting Quality in Schools and Colleges*. Educational Management Information Exchange. Slough: NFER.

Nixon, J. and Rudduck, J. (1993) The Role of Professional Judgement in the Local Inspection of Schools: a Study of Six Local Education Authorities. *Research Papers in Education*, 8, 1: 135–48.

Northam, J. (1993) *OFSTED's First Hundred: An Analysis of the Inspection Reports on One Hundred Primary and Secondary School Inspections*. Walpole House Associates, Occasional Paper No 1. Twickenham: St Mary's College.

OFSTED (1992a; 1993a; 1994a) *Framework for the Inspection of Schools*. London: OFSTED.

OFSTED (1992b) *Handbook for the Inspection of Schools*. London: OFSTED.

OFSTED (1993b; 1994b) *Handbook for the Inspection of Schools*. London: HMSO.

OFSTED (1993c) *Corporate Plan 1993–94 to 1995–96*. London: OFSTED.

OFSTED (1994c) *A Focus on Quality*. London: OFSTED.

OFSTED (1994d) *Improving Schools*. London: HMSO.

OFSTED (1995a) *Interim Guidance for Inspectors*. Update, 12. London: OFSTED.

OFSTED (1995b) *Inspection Quality 1994/95*. London: OFSTED.

OFSTED (1995c) *Revision of the Framework: National Consultation*. Update, 13. London: OFSTED.

OFSTED (1995d) *Planning Improvement: Schools' Post-Inspection Plans*. London: OFSTED.

OFSTED (1995e) *The First 200 Section 9 Inspections of Primary Schools*. London: OFSTED.

OFSTED (1995f) *Response to the New Framework*. Update, 15, Annex A. London: OFSTED.

OFSTED (1995g) *Guidance on the Inspection of Primary Schools*. London: HMSO.
OFSTED (1995h) *Guidance on the Inspection of Secondary Schools*. London: HMSO.
OFSTED (1995i) *Guidance on the Inspection of Special Schools*. London: HMSO.
Ouston, J. Fidler, B. and Earley, P. (eds) (1996) *OFSTED Inspection: The Early 'Experience'*. London: David Fulton.
Pearce, J. (1986a) School oversight in England and Wales. *European Journal of Education*, 21, 4: 331–44.
Pearce, J. (1986b) *Standards and the LEA: The Accountability of Schools*. Windsor: NFER Nelson.
Perry, P. (1995) The formation of OFSTED, in T. Brighouse and B. Moon (eds) *School Inspection*. London: Pitman Publishing.
Power, M. (1994) *The Audit Explosion*. London: DEMOS.
Power, M. and Laughlin, R. (1992) Critical theory and accounting, in M. Alvesson and H. Wilmott (eds) *Critical Management Studies*. London: Sage.
Roderick, R. (1986) *Habermas and the Foundations of Critical Theory*. Basingstoke: Macmillan.
Rorty, R. (1991) *Objectivity, Relativism, and Truth*. Cambridge: Cambridge University Press.
Sammons, P., Thomas, S., Mortimore, P., Owen, C. and Pennell, H. (1994) *Assessing School Effectiveness: Developing Measures to Put School Performance in Context*. London: London University Institute of Education for OFSTED.
SCAA (1994) *An Introduction to the Revised National Curriculum*. London: School Curriculum and Assessment Authority.
Sharp, M. (1992) Essex Man maligned. *Education*, 17 January: 55–6.
Silver, H. (1994) *Good Schools, Effective Schools*. London: Cassell.
Stillman, A. B. (1989) Institutional Evaluation and LEA Advisory Services. *Research Papers in Education*, 42, 2: 3–27.
Stillman, A. B. and Grant, M. (1989) *The LEA Adviser – A Changing Role*. Windsor: NFER Nelson.
Straw, J. (1991) *Raising the Standard: Labour's Plan for an Education Standards Commission*. London: The Labour Party.
Sutherland, S. (1992) Letter from HMCI-Designate enclosing a copy of the draft *Framework for Inspection*. London: DFE.
Times Educational Supplement (1995), 8 September: 16.
White, S. K. (1988) *The Recent Work of Jurgen Habermas: Reason, Justice and Modernity*. Cambridge: Cambridge University Press.
Wilcox, B. (1989) Inspection and its contribution to practical evaluation. *Educational Research*, 31, 3: 163–75.
Wilcox, B. (1992) *Time-Constrained Evaluation*. London: Routledge.
Wilcox, B. and Gray, J. (1995) The OFSTED inspection model: the views of LEA Chief Inspectors. *Cambridge Journal of Education*, 25, 1: 63–73.
Wilcox, B., Gray, J. and Tranmer, M. (1993) LEA frameworks for the assessment of schools: an interrupted picture. *Educational Research*, 35, 3: 211–21.
Wilson, T. A. (1995) Notes on the American fascination with the English tradition of school inspection. *Cambridge Journal of Education*, 25, 1: 89–96.
Wittgenstein, L. (1958) *Philosophical Investigations*. Oxford: Blackwell.
Wragg, E. C. and Brighouse, T. (1995) *A New Model of School Inspection*. Exeter: School of Education, Exeter University.

NAME INDEX

Stalker, H., 135, 143
Stillman, A.B., 28, 31, 36, 113
Straw, J., 32
Sutherland, S., 65, 81

Times Educational Supplement, 5

White, S.K., 123, 124
Wilcox, B., 6, 10, 31, 41, 144, 146

inspection as evaluation, 111, 115
school improvement, 47
survey of LEAs, 36
time, 123, 136
Wilson, T.A., 5, 116
Wittgenstein, L., 146
Woodhead, C., 132
Wragg, E.C., 7, 136

SUBJECT INDEX

'GOOD SCHOOL, BAD SCHOOL'
EVALUATING PERFORMANCE AND ENCOURAGING IMPROVEMENT

John Gray and Brian Wilcox

- How can one tell a 'good' school from a 'bad' one?
- How should schools be judged?
- How best might schools be improved?

Questions about the quality of schooling have dominated the political agenda for much of the past decade. As a direct result new policies have been introduced involving more performance indicators, league tables of exam results, more frequent inspection and the closure of 'failing' schools.

Studies of school effectiveness and school improvement have much to contribute to these questions. Drawing on the latest research, John Gray and Brian Wilcox take a fresh and critical look at some of the reforms. How can one ensure that a broader view of what education is about is retained in the face of narrow performance indicators? What contribution can value-added approaches make to ensuring that schools in disadvantaged areas are judged more fairly? How sound are inspection procedures? What happens after a school has been inspected? How much do schools actually improve over time? And what prospects are there for turning round 'failing' schools rather than simply closing them?

Contents
Introduction – Part 1: Setting frameworks – The quality of schooling: frameworks for judgement – Developing LEA frameworks for monitoring and evaluation from research on school effectiveness – Part 2: Gathering 'hard evidence' – HMI's interpretations of schools' examination results (with postscripts for the 1990s) – Performance indicators: flourish or perish – Developing value-added approaches to school evaluation: the experiences of three LEAs – Estimating differences in the examination performances of secondary schools in six LEAs: a multi-level approach to school effectiveness – Part 3: Inspection and school improvement: rhetoric and experience from the bridge – Reactions to inspection: a study of three variants – The methodologies of school inspection: issues and dilemmas – The inspectors recommended . . . a follow-up study in six secondary schools – Part 4: Looking to the future – The statistics of school improvement: establishing the agenda – The challenge of turning round ineffective schools – References – Subject index – Name index.

304pp   0 335 19489 3 (Paperback)   0 335 19490 7 (Hardback)

CHANGING OUR SCHOOLS
LINKING SCHOOL EFFECTIVENESS AND SCHOOL IMPROVEMENT
Louise Stoll and Dean Fink

Many of our schools are good schools – if this were 1965. Processes and structures designed for a time that has passed are no longer appropriate in a rapidly changing society. Throughout the world a great deal of effort and money has been expended in the name of educational change. Much of it has been misdirected and some of it wasteful. This book assists people inside and outside schools to bring about positive change by helping them to define the purposes behind change, the processes needed to achieve change and the results which they should expect. By linking the **why, what** and **how** of change, the authors provide a theoretical critique and practical advice to assist all those committed to changing and improving schools.

> Very few books on school reform contain so many ideas and insights while managing to construct a coherent and comprehensive message. Stoll and Fink have written an invaluable resource which is rich both conceptually and practically. This is a book that can be read in part or whole with great profit.
>
> Michael Fullan

Contents
Good schools if this were 1965: the context of change – The Halton Effective Schools Project: a story of change – School effectiveness can inform school improvement – The possibilities and challenges of school improvement – School development planning: a path to change – The power of school culture – Invitational leadership – Changing concepts of teaching and learning – The need for partnerships – Learning for all: building the learning community – Evaluate what you value – Changing our schools: linking school effectiveness and school improvement – References – Index.

240pp   0 335 19290 4 (Paperback)   0 335 19291 2 (Hardback)